"Years ago, my wife and I had the great benefit of learning about how wonderful a marriage can be from Ted Lowe and the amazing events he produced. That he's partnered with Doug Fields and created a book to help other marriages is absolutely awesome!"

—**Jon Acuff,** *New York Times* bestselling author
of *Start* and *Stuff Christians Like*

"If you think marriage ministry is outdated, boring, preachy or feminine, then please read *Married People*. Ted Lowe and Doug Fields do a masterful job of crafting a relevant, fun and engaging marriage ministry strategy for the local church. I know of no other book like it. My hope is that churches will implement their approach and everyone will be FOR marriage."

—**Ted Cunningham,** founding pastor, Woodland Hills Family
Church, Branson, Missouri, and author of *Fun Loving You*

"Every church is filled with couples struggling in their marriage. We want to help couples have an amazing marriage, but most of our time, resources, and energy are given as a reaction to marital crisis. What I love about *Married People* is the holistic vision it provides every church and pastor to gain influence with married people and create irresistible environments for them to grow in their love for God and each other. We can't change a human heart, but we can provide the space and opportunities for God to transform married couples. This is a must-have resource for all churches."

—**Justin Davis,** pastor, Cross Point Church, Nashville,
Tennessee, and co-author of *Beyond Ordinary: When
a Good Marriage Just Isn't Good Enough*

"Wow, I hope every church leader in America reads this important and helpful book. Marriage ministry in the church is one of those unusual areas where setting up just a few strategic things can make a big difference in the lives of those in the congregation. But church leaders are often so stretched, much of our ministry to marriages realistically ends up happening when trouble hits. Ted and Doug's book gives church leaders a vision and simple options for creating an ongoing marriage ministry structure that will prevent much of that trouble to begin with! I am excited to see this resource and know that every church implementing these well-thought-out and easy-to-use ideas will see a great blessing on marriages!"

—**Shaunti Feldhahn,** social researcher, speaker, and author of *For Women Only, For Men Only,* and *The Good News About Marriage*

"As culture shifts and marriages continue to struggle, the church at large is desperate to find its voice in engaging, equipping and empowering today's marriages. *Married People: How Your Church Can Build Marriages that Last* gives words to start conversations and reignite passion within the church to be a voice for this generation and generations to come."

—**Trisha Davis,** co-author of *Beyond Ordinary: When a Good Marriage Just Isn't Good Enough* and co-founder, RefineUs Ministries

"Ted and Doug provide a refreshing mix of theory, personal stories, humour and hyper-practical implementation tips. Plus, they get men. I can't wait to see this book unleashed on leaders and the church."

—**Carey Nieuwhof,** lead pastor, Connexus Church, Toronto

"Beyond the age of 18, the greatest opportunities for a person to come to faith through the local church are marriage, the birth of a child, or death. *Married People* is a principled-based, must-have resource for any marriage champion. Finally, a strategy to strengthen marriages and families inside the church that addresses felt-needs discipleship."

—**Tim Popadic,** national director, Date Night Works

"Every leader I know wants to better love and serve marriages. Finally a book that gives leaders the road map and practical tools they need to make a lifelong difference in couples and families."

—**Kara Powell,** executive director, Fuller Youth Institute

MARRIED PEOPLE

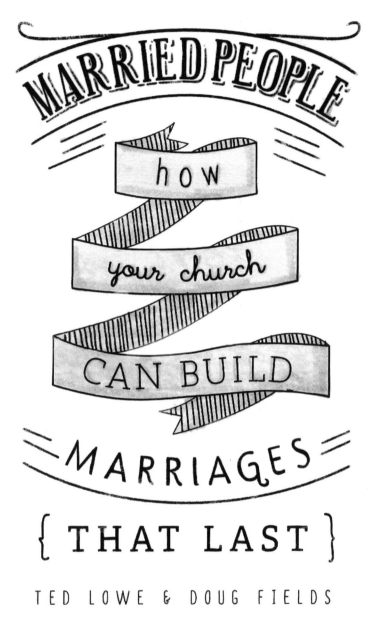

MARRIED PEOPLE

how your church CAN BUILD MARRIAGES { THAT LAST }

TED LOWE & DOUG FIELDS

orange

Married People
How Your Church Can Build Marriages that Last

Published by Orange, a division of The reThink Group, Inc.
5870 Charlotte Lane, Suite 300
Cumming, GA 30040 U.S.A.

The Orange logo is a registered trademark of The reThink Group, Inc.

Other Orange products are available online and direct from the publisher. Visit
OrangeBooks.com and ThinkOrange.com for more resources like these.

Website addresses and other sources of information listed throughout this book are
offered as resources to you. These resources are not intended in any way to be or
imply an endorsement on the part of The reThink Group, nor do we vouch for their
content.

Scripture marked "NIV" is taken from the Holy Bible, NEW INTERNATIONAL
VERSION®. Copyright © 1973, 1978, 1984 by Biblica, Inc. All rights reserved
worldwide. Used by permission.

Scripture marked "NCV" is taken from New Century Version®. Copyright © 2005
by Thomas Nelson, Inc. Used by permission. All rights reserved.

ISBN 978-0-9890213-2-6

Edited by Melanie Williams
Art direction by Ryan Boon
Cover design by Sharon van Rossum
Interior design by Hudson Phillips and Sharon van Rossum

Printed in the United States of America
First Edition 2014, Reprinted 2015

2 3 4 5 6 7 8 9 10 11

04/12/2016

I dedicate this book to you, Nancie Lowe. I wrote this dedication in the middle of writing the book, and not only because I'm ADHD. I wrote it the middle because that is exactly where you have always been with me: in the middle. When I left an amazing job to start MarriedPeople, you were in the middle. As we continue to build MarriedPeople, you are in the middle. As I am writing this book, you are in the middle. You are always in the middle with me, full of support, encouragement, laughter, and perspective. If this book leads churches to help couples grow closer to God and each other, it's because you were in the middle of writing of it. I love doing life with you … in the middle.

Ted

There's a saying that goes like this: "The best thing about me is you." This is totally true of my family. Cathy, 30 years have gone by so fast because life is so rich when I'm with you. Our marriage inspires me to want others to experience what we have, most importantly our own children. I dedicate this book to Torie, Cody, and Cassie Fields and your future spouses. I pray daily that you marry someone like your mom so that the Fieldses' legacy continues.

Doug

CONTENTS

FOREWORD

I am writing this a week before my oldest daughter's wedding day. She is only one of two million who will get married this year. But she's different from the rest. She's my daughter. I could pretend I care about everyone else's marriage as much as I do hers. But I don't. I guess because as a parent, you just feel things more deeply and strongly when it involves your own child. That's why I feel compelled to ask you this question first as a parent: **Do you have a plan to help marriages in your church grow stronger?**

I'm not asking if you have a book, or a sermon series, or a workshop, or a small group study for couples. There are more resources than ever before available to help marriages. But there is a difference between providing information and having a clear, strategic plan to help couples consistently fight for their relationship.

So let me ask the question another way: **If my daughter and her new husband moved to your city, could you explain your weekly, monthly, and yearly plan to help them stay in a dynamic and growing relationship with each other?**

That's why this book was written. Ted and Doug are not only asking you that question as parents; they are asking you as pastors and leaders. Well over half the adults in any given community are married, and nearly 80 percent of them don't attend church. That's why when your church becomes an advocate for marriage, it makes a powerful and positive statement to people inside and outside your church.

When you implement a clear strategy about marriage church-wide, it affects the spiritual health of every couple who attends your church. It provides a model for future generations who happen to be watching. It sends a message to every unchurched couple in your community. (By the way, it also suggests that you actually care about what happens in the one relationship that is usually most important to a husband or wife.)

Here's another question I would like for you to consider: **If your church doesn't do this in your community, who will?**

Your city government?

The private or public schools in your area?

Random counselors and therapists?

Think about it. Who in your community has the best opportunity to inspire couples to influence other couples to build stronger marriages? There are a lot of us who believe the answer to that question is the church. That's why *Married People* is not just another book about how to build a great marriage. Instead, **it's a book about how to gain influence with married people**. We think the stakes are really high, and that there needs to be a renewed effort to help couples win.

If you haven't had an effective plan to this point for married couples in your church, you do now. Doug Fields and Ted Lowe have spent decades implementing a practical and strategic style of ministry. They have reputations for being impatient with programs that don't lead anywhere and teaching that doesn't engage anyone. These pages are filled with insights from seasoned pastors on how to leverage the church's influence and platforms to make marriages successful. Fields and Lowe have done the work for the rest of us; now it's our turn to respond. So read this book carefully. Then we hope you will analyze, customize, and personalize the ideas in it for your church and community.

Because someone's recently married daughter and her husband could be moving to your city. They just need you to take some time and make a plan to help their marriage win.

Reggie Joiner, Founder and President, Orange

DON'T
SKIP
This Part

MARRIED PEOPLE

FINISH THIS STORY

Beth Johnson stood at the kitchen window and watched her husband, Blake, drive away for the last time before their divorce was to be finalized. Once his car was out of view, she braced herself against the counter and sobbed. She stopped crying almost as quickly as she had started because she knew the kids would soon be home from school.

Blake was typically strong and composed, so he was surprised his hands were shaking. He pulled into the parking lot of the neighborhood clubhouse, where other parents were parked to meet their children's school bus. He regretted his decision to pull over when he saw Maria, a neighbor who always picked up his kids on Thursdays. Maria got out of her car and walked over to Blake. He lowered his window.

"Is everything okay?" Maria asked.

"Yes," Blake said. "I'm just picking up the girls because ... uh, well ... I'm taking the afternoon off from work."

"Oh, that's great. The girls will be thrilled."

Blake nodded, ending the awkward conversation by quickly raising the window. Now his hands were really shaking. But why? After all, the divorce was the best thing for everyone, especially the kids, right?

As he waited, he once again began to think through everything he and Beth had tried to make their marriage work. They had seen a counselor three times. They had attended the church marriage retreat. Most of their friends agreed divorce was the right move. What else could they have done? Just then the bus drove up and the girls got off and ran to his car, a little confused to see their dad there on a Thursday, but excited nonetheless. The short ride home was filled with stories about recess and how the eggs in the incubator at school had finally hatched the "cutest chicks in the whole wide world."

Beth was shocked when she saw Blake pull into the driveway with the girls. Blake stopped the car and wondered if he should make a quick exit or allow the girls to get settled first. Beth wondered what he was doing. A small part of her questioned whether he had changed his mind. No way! That wasn't possible. They were both certain. Right? The fighting in front of the kids had to stop. It was better for them to grow up in two peaceful homes rather than one chaotic one. Right?

Beth hesitated, then went outside. The girls got out of the car. Jenny, the spitting image of Beth, turned and said, "Get out of the car, Daddy! Mommy, the eggs hatched at school!"

Sara headed straight into the house. She had been quiet and distant for months. Blake and Beth both knew Sara realized something was not right with their marriage. As Sara went by, Beth said, "Hi, baby, how was your day?" Without breaking stride Sara mumbled, "Fine" and continued to her room.

Dancing around the driveway, firecracker Jenny said, "Daddy, why did you meet us at the bus? Jake's mom always meets us on Thursdays." She ran and grabbed him by the hand to pull him out of the car. Blake didn't move. The situation had left him feeling like deadweight. "Get out, Daddy. Let's play. Jump on the trampoline with me."

"No, Jenny. I have to go."

"Go where?" she asked.

"Honey, I have … I have to go back to work and I need to …" His voice trailed off.

Jenny's face went from exuberant to flat in a millisecond. What had appeared to be a great surprise on a random Thursday was now just a big disappointment.

"Go ahead, Jenny," Beth said. "Go inside. Daddy needs to go." Jenny didn't move.

Blake was taken aback by the way Beth said "Daddy"; no sarcasm, no contempt. Seeing Beth and Jenny standing there together, looking just alike, felt like torture. "Beth, can we talk for just a minute?" Blake was as surprised as Beth to hear those words coming from his mouth.

"Don't you need to get back to work?"

"Yes, but it will only take a minute. Jenny, can you give your mom and me just a few minutes by ourselves?" Jenny kicked the ground and ran inside.

Then Blake said …

/////

Let's hit pause on the Johnsons' story.

KEY QUESTIONS THIS FAMILY NEEDS CHURCH LEADERS TO WRESTLE WITH

How do you think their story will end? What is Blake likely to say? How will Beth respond at this point? A better question might be, how would you like this story to end, or at least to re-begin? What would happen if Blake and Beth were regular attendees at your church?

That brings up additional important questions for us as church leaders:

1. What does Scripture really say about what the church's role is when it comes to helping Beth, Blake, Sara, and Jenny?
2. To what extent should the church feel responsible when it comes to empowering all marriages, whether they are struggling, barely surviving, or even growing and healthy?
3. If the church is intentional about strengthening marriages, will it send an alienating message to those who aren't yet married, or who never want to be married?
4. There is only so much time and only so many resources. Does the church let another area of ministry slide in order to help marriages?
5. If we don't do what we can to strengthen marriages, what does that do to the growth and health of our church?
6. Is our church's attempt to help marriages working?
7. Is marriage really the church's business? If not, whose is it?
8. What might result if our church chooses not to be aggressive in helping marriages?

9. What would God have our church do to help build marriages that last?

FROM GREAT QUESTIONS COME ... MORE QUESTIONS

With ministry moving at the speed of light, we wondered how many leaders would pause long enough to consider these kinds of questions when it comes to how our churches approach marriage. Thankfully, you are one of many; there is a wave of marriage awareness building among church leaders.

These leaders believe, or are starting to believe, that it is absolutely the church's role to help Beth, Blake, Sara, and Jenny. They are realizing that the time to equip couples through the local church is now. They are seeing the need to intersect with the lives of married couples long before the point their marriages are likely to come apart. They are sensing that while marriage is messy and comes with a lot of baggage and sensitivity, they can no longer ignore the mess.

Even though they are busy creating programs and sermons and all manner of content every week, they are beginning to consider that maybe changes need to be made in order to make marriage a priority. They are having meetings (sometimes awkward ones) in order to ask whether what they are doing to help married couples is working. As kids flood the church each week, they are wondering what hangs in the balance for these children if they simply let nature take its course with their parents' marriages. In terms of tithing, attendance, and volunteerism, it is becoming clearer every day that, practically speaking, the growth and the health of their church depends greatly on how they answer this question: How do we empower marriages?

While these thoughts and questions are not easy to digest, the benefits that come from the answers (and from the hard work of digging for answers) are nothing short of life altering for the health of individual families, the local church, and society as a whole. What if the church could really get this empowering married couples thing right? The implications are massive.

WHERE WE ARE HEADED (AND WHAT THIS BOOK WILL DO FOR YOU)

Because you are reading this book, we are guessing you not only care about marriages, you care about the church "being the church" to people. That is, people relating to others in ways that strengthen one another's marriages and make it less likely that couples will call it quits. We are also betting you have some good ideas for how to get there, but haven't been able to implement them for one reason or another. Or, it may be you feel overwhelmed at the thought of creating and implementing such a ministry. We've been there, and thankfully, we've been staring at these kinds of questions long enough that we are at a point to help answer them.

While we hope this book inspires you with God's purposes and plan for marriage, we also pray that, in a relatively short amount of time, this book gives you …

- A proactive strategy to strengthen all marriages.
- Practical steps for launching and implementing the strategy.
- Principles and steps you can employ if you want to develop your own strategy.
- Tools to impact marriages, both in and outside the church, while strengthening your church in the process.

- A marriage ministry "manual" that you can come back to again and again.

People have asked if this book is for married couples. We say yes, it is, but not in the usual way. The purpose of this book (and the heart and passion behind it) is to equip churches to help build marriages that last. While that may sound idealistic, the way we hope to help you accomplish that will actually be very practical.

We are honored you are reading this book. But more than that, we are excited that you might join us and become a pioneer in the movement to minister to married people. We are thrilled with this new tribe of people in the church who are passionate about the local church helping marriages, and who want the church to be known as THE place in the community that strengthens marriages. You are about to enter into something rewarding and life changing. Buckle up and let's go.

CHAPTER
ONE

Three
BIG REASONS
why
MARRIAGE
Is the Church's
Business

MARRIED PEOPLE

{ ONE }

PARTY CRASHER

Recently my wife, Nancie, and I (Ted) were attending a party in our daughter's second grade class. The room was packed with parents, some sitting in tiny chairs as they watched a barely visible photo slide show, others walking around oohing and ahhing over accidental abstract art. Despite the bedlam, Nancie noticed a little girl whose parents either had yet to arrive or weren't coming. Nancie walked over and engaged her in conversation, complimenting the child on her "amazing" artwork. As they talked, Nancie asked her a seemingly harmless question: "Do you have any brothers or sisters?" The child said, "Yes, I have one sister, but she lives in Louisiana with my daddy." Then she said something that is still ringing in my ears, "We are a divorce." Nancie's facial expression changed in a way that only I noticed, but those telling words, "We are a divorce," broke her heart as much as it did mine.

Like you, we hate that phrase, but we're confident we have some real answers for churches that want to help people avoid these circumstances—answers that offer hope as well as practical help. But before we jump into the "how," let's spend a short amount of time addressing the "why" behind the need for the church's involvement in marriage.

We believe there are three compelling reasons why marriage is absolutely the church's business.

REASON #1:
MARRIAGE IS THE CHURCH'S BUSINESS BECAUSE KIDS NEED A LOVING MOM AND DAD IN THE HOME

We bet you have your own version of "we are a divorce." Maybe it's your child's best friend whose parents have gotten a divorce. Maybe some of your own friends, a co-worker, or your parents are divorced. Perhaps you've been through divorce yourself. Despite the common nature of divorce today, it hurts as much as ever, and the consequences trigger pain that echoes for years.

Research indicates that children, regardless of socio-economic status, whose parents divorce are more likely than kids from intact marriages to drop out of high school, get pregnant, and **spend time in prison**.[1] They are more likely to **start smoking**[2] and to be **susceptible to illness**.[3] They may also run a **greater risk for divorce themselves**.[4] We are absolutely *not* saying that children of divorced parents are doomed to these outcomes; however, if these things come true for even a few of the children in your church's care, that would be reason enough to pay attention to their parents' marriages, wouldn't it?

Besides, divorce is not the only thing that tears the fabric of marriage and family. Consider the impact on the children of a couple going through economic hardship, abuse, neglect, infidelity, addiction, problem drinking—anything that undermines stability in the home is difficult enough for the adults, but even more so for the children, who need stability in order to thrive.

When these situations weigh heavily on our hearts, it's easy to get pumped up and passionate about the church's role in keeping homes together. Helping to minimize family pain, regardless of the programs or ministries through which that happens, requires the church's best energy. Maybe intact homes in which moms and dads love each other is a good enough reason for the church to help marriages, but we don't think it's the underlying reason. You might be thinking, *What could be more important than a loving and supportive home?* Keep reading.

REASON #2:
MARRIAGE IS THE CHURCH'S BUSINESS BECAUSE IT'S AN ILLUSTRATION OF JESUS AND HIS CHURCH

Churches should actively support marriages because marriage reflects the relationship between Jesus and His church.

> **Husbands, love your wives, just as Christ loved the church and gave himself up for her to make her holy, cleansing her by the washing with water through the word, and to present her to himself as a radiant church, without stain or wrinkle or any other blemish, but holy and blameless. (Ephesians 5:25-27, NIV)**

We're willing to wager (in a non-gambling sort of way, of course) that most married couples don't think of marriage as a mirror-like image of the relationship Christ has with His church, but the Apostle Paul says it is.

You can bet Paul got the Ephesians' attention when he told them that husbands should view their wives the way Jesus views the church. He said a husband should love his wife as he loves himself and do everything in his power to care for her and build her up. In other words, marriage should mean more to a man than satisfying his own desires. It should be more about what he can (and should) do for his wife than for himself.

If Jesus is doing everything He can to build up the church that bears His name (and He is), then it stands to reason that the church ought to be doing everything it can to ensure that marriages are strong. Strong, healthy marriages in the church benefit the couples involved as well as present an attractive example to outsiders, some of whom have never seen a truly healthy and godly marriage up close.

This concept became the primary focus of our early teaching on marriage. We'd say (and still believe) that marriage reflects the relationship between Christ and the church. So here are two big questions that should rattle our cage, church leaders:

- What do the marriages in your church say about *Jesus*?
- What do the marriages in your church say about your *church*?

In today's **weakening marital culture**,[5] strong marriages are highly attractive to people. And for those who are followers of Jesus, a marriage that is working well can point back to the relationship between Christ and the church. (One could hypothesize that Mormonism's biggest draw is the way it portrays its people, "living advertisements" for community, family, and marriage.)

However, this isn't the central reason we think churches should be intentional about helping marriages either.

REASON #3:
MARRIAGE IS THE CHURCH'S BUSINESS BECAUSE MARRIAGE IS A SPIRITUAL ISSUE

While we believe children need intact homes and marriage reflects the relationship between Jesus and the church, the primary reason we felt compelled to write this book is that marriage is a spiritual issue.

Think about it …

When marriage isn't working, it robs us of our best relationship with God.

For example, imagine a morning in which you and your spouse argue over one of those issues that seems so big at the time, but is so dumb upon reflection. You know the type: leaving a towel on the floor, misplacing a credit card receipt, or saying (with a little "tone"), "Why can't *you* take care of that?" Now imagine that small issue sparks enough emotion to provide ammunition for a big fight. And after that big fight, picture yourself heading off somewhere to have quiet time with God. How do you envision that working for you?

Right. If you're a normal human, you'll most likely find it difficult to connect with God when you are at odds with the person you're "one flesh" with. Why? Easy answer—it's because marriage is a spiritual issue.

Furthermore …

Marriage, by its very nature, is transformative.

Consider how marriage changes things. Let's go back to those examples above. If you are tidy and your spouse is messy, this radically impacts the likelihood of your living in an orderly home. If you are a spender and your spouse is a saver, this reality will profoundly change the way you deal with money. If you are the type who rarely uses the pause feature of your mouth, and your spouse is a sensitive soul, this will drastically affect … well, pretty much everything. You get the point: marriage brings about transformation.

This is even truer for people who align their lives with the person and teachings of Jesus. As disciples, we are called to love our spouses in radical ways: We are to put their needs ahead of our own. We are to limit our sexual desires to them only. We are to forgive them as Jesus has forgiven us. This kind of love is counter-cultural, even supernatural.

In fact …

There is, perhaps, no greater relationship that God uses to make us more like Him than marriage.

While most relationships have a seasonal element to them, marriage is intended to last until death. (See Hosea 2:19-20 and Matthew 19:4-6.) Work relationships come and go, as do friends, neighbors, and mentors. Even the nature of parent-child and sibling relationships changes significantly over time. But God's intentions for marriage are steeper. As a result, marriage enjoys a unique status, one marked by choice, commitment, and exclusivity. We don't choose our family, co-workers, and neighbors, but we do choose and commit to a spouse. Apart from our relationship with Jesus, **what relationship other than marriage**[6] has the most potential to draw us closer to God, over a longer period of time?

Reading between the lines, Paul is acknowledging the extraordinary nature of marriage when he focuses on that relationship in Ephesians 5:21-33. (The only other specific relationships he addresses in this passage are parent-child [understandable] and slave-master [another topic for another time].) Perhaps he is also underscoring the idea that a fundamental purpose of marriage is similar to that of the church: to make us more like Jesus.

That idea could radically alter the way people approach marriage. As Gary Thomas so beautifully points out in his book *Sacred Marriage*, what if marriage is more about us being transformed into the likeness and character of Jesus than about **our desire for comfort, happiness, or self-fulfillment?**[7] What if marriage, through its joys and difficulties, was the perfect soil for growing the fruit of God's Spirit: love, joy, peace, patience, kindness, goodness, faithfulness, gentleness, and self-control? And what if God intended spouses to be the primary beneficiaries of that fruit?

That view changes everything. It should also change how we approach ministry to married couples.

MINISTRY TO MARRIED PEOPLE IS A "HAVE TO"

We can debate which of the above is the most compelling reason the church should be deliberate in its ministry to married couples. You might even have other reasons that are every bit as convincing.

For instance, you could argue that when marriages are in trouble, the church is in trouble. (Weak marriages = weaker involvement in volunteerism, worship, attendance, and tithing.) You could argue the point from the positive view as well: when marriages are going great, the church is going great. (Strong marriages = stronger involvement in volunteerism, worship, attendance, and tithing.)

Or, for you it may be as much about marriages outside the church as in the church. You might convince us that caring for people's marriages in intentional, strategic ways is one of the greatest tools available to the church—not just for discipling insiders, but for reaching outsiders. You see empowering couples as an amazing opportunity to bridge the church and culture: empowering marriages inside and outside the church affects kids, affects how people view the church, and affects people spiritually, all of which impacts culture.

Regardless of why you think churches should strengthen and empower marriages, most of us would probably agree that we should. Ministry to married couples is a have to if we want to impact our congregations and attract a hurting world. And if it's a have to, then we need to be excellent at our approach. That's what this book is all about: helping all of us who care about marriages to approach ministry in a way that makes a real difference. Let's begin the process by asking the question: Where are we in our ministry to married couples?

{ chapter
TWO }

marriage MINISTRY in the local church: WHERE ARE WE?

MARRIED PEOPLE

{TWO}

ARE WE THERE YET?

In National Lampoon's movie *Vacation*, Clark Griswold (played by Chevy Chase) dreams of the perfect family vacation with his wife, son, and daughter. He plans in great detail every stop of the cross-country trip, particularly the final stop at Walley World Amusement Park. The road trip is actually one disappointment after another. But Clark holds out hope that once they get to Walley World, all the bad will be forgotten. When they finally arrive, they park the car and run to the entrance only to be greeted by an animatronics moose that says: "Sorry, folks, we're closed for two weeks to clean and repair America's family fun park. Sorry." Clark punches the moose in total frustration.

If you took a trip to find "Marriage Ministry World," chances are your search would be one disappointment after another, ultimately discovering that, for many churches, Marriage Ministry

World doesn't really exist. Like us, you may have even wished for a "moose" to punch.

The great news is there is a Marriage Ministry World being built. In fact, we want you to be some of the first ones to join us in its construction. But first, let's take a quick trip to see what the church is currently doing to help marriages.

GOOD AND BAD NEWS

The good news is that we don't have to convince many church leaders to deconstruct their old ways of doing marriage ministry because many churches don't have much of a marriage ministry. Or, if they do, it's something of a Band-Aid-type approach they're not fully committed to. In other words, they have a clean slate or can start over fairly easily.

The bad news is that most churches don't have much of a marriage ministry, which means they may have precious little budget and leadership in place with which to do something about it.

While many churches attempt to help marriages (through small group studies, retreats, and pointed sermon series), it's simply not enough. We need models and mentors and leaders to start a marriage movement. And, unlike many previous niche ministries, there are few church-based models leading the way. Most people we talk to assume it's the largest churches that "do more" for marriages, but that's **not an accurate assumption**.[8]

WELL, WHAT IS THE CHURCH DOING FOR MARRIAGES?

Based on our observation and study of churches doing anything in the marriage space, most take one of three different approaches when it comes to reaching married couples: (1) an indirect approach; (2) a reactionary approach; or (3) a topical approach. Each approach often has a set of assumptions, or myths, associated with it. Let's take a quick look at each approach and some related myths and see why these current models fall short of what's possible.

APPROACH #1: THE INDIRECT APPROACH

Churches take an indirect approach when they continue "business as usual" under the supposition that their current efforts are enough to help marriages. We see this assumption revealed through several different myths.

The myth of "Sunday morning is enough!"

This seems to be a common notion among churches that take an indirect approach to marriage ministry, perhaps, in part, because the pace of ministry can be so demanding that there's little time to stop and think. In order to develop an effective ministry to married couples, church leadership must be able to wind down the "ministry machine" long enough to reflect and ask significant questions like, What can and should our church be doing to help the marriages that God has entrusted to our care?

Busy leaders tend to get defensive when they hear us talk like this. We heard this comment at a recent conference, "We have a ministry to married couples every week; it's called our *worship service*. If you teach the Word of God on Sunday mornings, and people apply it to their lives, it will improve their marriages."

There's no doubt that statement is true. We're champions of God's Word as the final authority when it comes to marriage, and weekly corporate worship is important to both faith and marriage. But the attitude behind that statement overlooks the fact that many couples sitting in churches every week have big-time hurts that are specific to their marriage. It's difficult to think about loving their neighbor when they don't even *like* their spouse. What may be even worse is their belief that they are the only ones struggling in a room full of people. Feeling alone, yet surrounded by fellow strugglers who don't want to admit their pain, is a terrible place to sit.

Surprisingly, struggling people can feel alone even when the preacher/teacher/speaker shares a story about his or her own marital difficulty. Personal pain seems to weaken one's ability to engage and hear what's actually being said. Countless times we've spoken to a crowd and shared a personal struggle within our marriages, and without fail, someone will make a comment afterward like, "I bet you have the perfect marriage." *Really? Weren't you in the room just now? Or did you take a bathroom break during that story of pain, fighting, and frustration?* Nope. They were there; their own pain created a momentary deafness.

This is one reason we need to do more for marriages than simply preach a message every week, hoping it helps. We need something stronger than a strategy based on hope alone.

The myth of "Marriage is about getting MY needs met."

Another reason we can't rely on an indirect approach to strengthen marriages is that many married people in our churches have a fundamentally flawed view of marriage, one that the church needs to address directly. These couples haven't necessarily chosen it, but they have adopted it from culture or learned it from their families. They, like their church leaders, are so busy that they don't have time to think and reflect deeply about marriage.

This faulty view of marriage has left many in a constant state of frustration. Brad Wilcox (director of the National Marriage

Project at the University of Virginia) calls it the "soul-mate model" of marriage: "Prior to the late 1960s, Americans were more likely to look at marriage and family through the prisms of duty, obligation, and sacrifice …. But the psychological revolution's focus [of the '60s and '70s] on individual fulfillment and personal growth changed all that. Increasingly, marriage was seen as a vehicle for a **self-oriented ethic of romance, intimacy, and fulfillment**." [9] While many people may enter marriage wishing it was all about them, they quickly discover otherwise.

People who believe the purpose of marriage is to meet their needs or to sustain constant romantic feelings are more likely than not to be disappointed and frustrated in marriage. These discouraged couples fill our churches. This creates an awesome responsibility, opportunity, and privilege for the church to step up and paint a clearer and bigger picture of God's ideal for marriage.

The myth of "We will alienate people if we focus on marriage."

Another reason churches take an indirect approach to ministering to married couples isn't a reason at all; it's a fear. Many church leaders fear that if they really address marriage, which includes addressing it during corporate worship, they will alienate or marginalize large portions of their audience, such as single parents, the widowed, or those who don't want to get married. We totally understand that concern. When I (Ted) was a kid, I learned that "everyone" at church spoke as if all kids had a mom. But I didn't! (My mom died when I was 10.) In fact, that's why my dad never made me go to church on Mother's Day. In the same way, we NEVER, ever want a ministry to married couples to make anyone feel left out or judged for not being married.

However, it's very easy to have a full-throttle ministry to married couples without hurting those who aren't married. Here's a simple but absolutely essential guideline to keep in mind: **When you are focusing on marriage, you have to acknowledge and empower everyone.** For example, your pastor might say something like this to introduce a message: "Today, we are focusing on a marriage principle because marriage is important to everyone in the room. That, of course, includes those of you who are married, but it also includes those of you who want to marry, or want to remarry, one day. It's also important to all parents, whether your kids are 22 or 42. Because even if you are a single parent, you are the one responsible for equipping your kids when it comes to their marriage." Again, we simply need to acknowledge everyone in the room, and then give them applications and examples that make sense in their world. It's that easy, but that essential.

Regardless of the reason churches may take an indirect approach to ministering to married couples, it is not a viable one for churches that truly want to impact families and the next generation.

APPROACH #2: THE REACTIONARY APPROACH

Churches taking a reactionary approach to marriage ministry primarily respond to the expressed needs of couples in crisis. In other words, the majority of their efforts to strengthen marriages is in direct response to a call for help, and as a result, is often late in the process. These churches have typically bought in to myths like the following.

The myth of "Couples will call when they need us."

Despite the fact that many churches aren't doing much "officially" to help marriages, many churches are directing some time and resources in reactionary ways. When struggling couples finally get around to approaching a church leader for help, presumably most leaders don't say, "Yeah, we're not really into the whole 'helping marriages thing.' Good luck with that. We'll be praying for you." We've had enough conversations with church leaders (including senior pastors) to know they will find time in their busy schedules to try to help couples in crisis.

This is admirable. We love to see pastoral gifts being put into action to aid the brokenhearted. But unless your church is truly equipped with lay people or professionals who know how to help couples at the breaking point, perhaps the best thing you can do is recommend qualified counselors outside the church. If the money is available and the couple is willing, this might be the wisest response in most situations. But the stigma and financial burden often associated with counseling are hurdles many couples simply can't clear.

The myth of "It's never too late."

While we believe God can work miracles at any time, there are some people who aren't open to God's intervention, or anyone else's. Unfortunately, there is often the "too late" factor that becomes an obstacle in counseling. Ever wonder why goodhearted pastors and (even) trained counselors have a tough time saving couples in crisis? Brian D. Doss (associate professor of psychology at the University of Miami) says couples wait an average of six years before they seek counseling, and by then it's often a last-ditch effort to fix a relationship **beyond repair**.[10] Thomas Bradbury (professor of psychology at the University of California, Los Angeles) likens a couple with marital problems to a person with a broken leg. If they get help right away, there's every chance they'll heal. But if they wait, a full recovery is almost impossible. By that time, "the therapist has to attend not only to the psychological equivalent of the broken bone, 'but also to the swelling and bruising, the sore hip and foot, and **the infection that ensued**.'"[11]

The problem with the reactionary approach is that by the time most couples seek help, it's often too late. Many have already decided on divorce as their only viable option and have simply added "talk to someone from church" as part of their pre-divorce checklist. Then, once they've met with "church people" a couple of times, they have the freedom to say, "We tried everything; we even talked to a leader at church." In counseling terms, this is referred to as a "therapist-endorsed divorce." In our terms, it's a "church-endorsed divorce." How do the words "church-endorsed divorce" hit you? If you are like us, you want to hit back.

We need to help couples in crisis; in fact, we believe it should be a part of your overall marriage strategy and one of the primary reasons we wrote this book. But what if there was another approach that could help couples avoid these almost-insurmountable crisis points in the first place? There is! (You'll read about it in the next chapter.)

APPROACH #3: THE TOPICAL APPROACH

Churches that take a topical approach to helping married couples view marriage as a "topic to be addressed." Many of these churches may assume the following to be true: **the myth of "We can fix marriages with one big concentrated effort."**

What do churches typically do when they want to address a topic or a concern? They'll teach about it—because it's tempting to think we can teach our way out of trouble. So, "topical" churches will have a one-off marriage sermon (or even a marriage sermon

Quite simply, **larger group experiences**[18] are the perfect context to get new people to your church. Larger group experiences inspire people to make *little* changes that provide *big* results. They also help couples like Ben and Cassandra experience a "marriage-thing" and actually want to come back.

{ CHAPTER
five }

EMPOWERING

small

GROUP

experiences

{ five }

STEPPING UP

For the first time in their marriage, **Jeremy and Tiffany Lee**[19] were at such a low place that divorce was becoming a real possibility, something they had said they would never even joke about. Tiffany recalls the morning after they separated: she'd called one of Jeremy's best friends, Rick, to tell him that Jeremy had moved out. Rick was shocked and sickened by the news and told her, "You two are NOT getting divorced. God is bigger than all of this …" That was on a Tuesday.

On Thursday night, Rick met with the Lees' closest friends to pray and talk through ideas to keep the two together. After a couple hours of prayer and discussion, they decided they were only going to "support the marriage"; they wouldn't support the option of divorce in any way. They established boundaries in which they wouldn't allow Jeremy or Tiffany to vent to them in a destructive nature. If Jeremy or Tiffany voiced something negative about each other, the response was to be: "Yes, she/he did that. You need to address that with her/him and your counselor." The counselor reinforced this approach, telling the couple to be careful who they talked to about their spouse and marriage; if at any point they found themselves having to defend their spouse to another person, "stop talking to that person about your marriage."

Let's pause the Lees' story for a moment. How does it make you feel? Does this story seem radical or refreshing to you? Think about it: What kind of people jump into an imploding marriage and attempt to save it? Do real humans actually say things like, "As your friends, we want to help you revive your marriage"? The answer is yes! This is the response from people who love and follow Jesus and are committed to one another. This group of friends stepped up and got involved in the Lees' relational *business*, and it worked for this couple.

Two years later, the Lees have a different kind of marriage and would tell you they are now happier than ever. And while their counselor deserves a lot of the credit, they'd confess that it was their friends' support, initiative, and belief that had the more dramatic impact. When we asked Jeremy and Tiffany to share their story, their memorable words were, "Surround yourselves with people who are for your *marriage*, not just people who are for *you*."

When you hear a story like this, you've got to wonder how many divorced couples would still be together if they had been surrounded by people who were "for their marriage." Here's the question for you and your church: How many couples in your church may stay together if you help surround them with people who are for their marriage? Jeremy and Tiffany's story needn't be the minority example; getting couples into healthy small groups that are "for the marriage" can enhance those odds.

Small groups not only can help protect marriages from divorce, they can also be instrumental in making good or even marginal marriages great. Yes, divorce destroys families, but so does abuse, neglect, infidelity, and any other action that springs from a wicked and wounded heart. When God's people come together and actually begin to care whether others learn and follow the ways of Jesus, amazing things can happen in a life and, therefore, a marriage. Surrounding marriages with couples who are for marriage can be great for *every* marriage.

RESULTS OF HEALTHY SMALL GROUP EXPERIENCES

There are several helpful books written on the how-to's of small groups that you can study if you need help in the practical application of the how. In this chapter, our goal is to paint a few broad strokes of what a small group looks like that is "for marriages."

Healthy small groups produce many positive outcomes for married couples. Here are just a few.

SMALL GROUPS CREATE COMMUNITY

And let us consider how we may spur one another on toward love and good deeds, not giving up meeting together, as some are in the habit of doing, but encouraging one another—and all the more as you see the Day approaching. (Hebrews 10:24-25, NIV)

These ancient verses describe perfectly the context that saved Tiffany and Jeremy's marriage. They met together often, they spurred each other toward love and good deeds, they didn't give up on meeting together, they encouraged one another. What a beautiful picture of Jesus followers doing life together in a context that is "for" marriage. As leaders, when we plant married people in the soil of healthy community, we can expect relational growth. Genuine friendships change people. Laughing together, shedding tears, revealing hopes and fears—these are the things that happen in a loving community. People quickly learn that we are better together. What a motivation—not to mention privilege—to help couples connect into groups.

SMALL GROUPS PROMOTE ACCOUNTABILITY

Therefore confess your sins to each other and pray for each other so that you may be healed. The prayer of a righteous person is powerful and effective. (James 5:16, NIV)

While confession and prayer may seem like ethereal concepts, small groups are often the setting in which confession and prayer become very real parts of one's faith. Consider how practical Tiffany and Jeremy's friends' prayers became: "Help us respond in ways that will support their marriage, not tear it apart." When Tiffany and Jeremy confessed to their friends, their honesty and wounding were met with love and support and a force of accountability that wouldn't allow either person to complain about the other. That's powerful. A small group is not just about having people to do life with; it's about having people in your life who want to help you live the life God desires for His people and who will be there to walk with you and hold you accountable to your commitments when it gets tough.

SMALL GROUPS STIMULATE FAITH

I mean that I want us to help each other with the faith we have. Your faith will help me, and my faith will help you. (Romans 1:12, NCV)

A smaller, more intimate setting not only helps people learn about Jesus and His ways, it also encourages people to live out that knowledge. A smaller group makes it difficult to hide and pretend to be someone you're not.

A recent Barna study compared people's church attendance and their "personal spiritual activities," like reading the Bible on their own. Most church attendees (67%) who participated in the study said they had read the Bible outside of church in the previous week. While that's exciting, those in small groups (84%) were even more likely to have read the Bible outside of church—more than any other group, including church volunteers and Sunday school **attendees**.[20] If a small group environment is a major catalyst for promoting spiritual maturity, it seems like a no-brainer for church leaders to implement small groups.

Bigger is not always better when it comes to discipleship. While Jesus did speak to the masses, He also chose 12 people on whom to focus His attention and launched a worldwide movement through that small group. He did it through loving them, leading them, and teaching them concretely and creatively. Now we get the opportunity to do the same thing.

HOW TO MAKE SMALL GROUPS MORE APPEALING

Many people are fearful of joining a small group. It you've ever been in a bad small group, you know some of those fears are valid. But a commitment to connect couples into small groups is something we encourage every church to do. Because once people taste authentic small group life (with accountability, community, and faith), they're usually in for life. The "experienced" are typically satisfied customers, but for those who have never tasted ... well, that's a different story. It's not always easy to talk people into a small group.

Here's the resistance we've experienced.

THE GUY FACTOR

As you may have discovered for yourself, men in particular resist marriage-type events and experiences. I (Ted) recently tried to convince a guy that he and his wife should participate in a weekend marriage intensive at a local retreat center. I shared with him the miraculous results these types of retreats are having. He was very interested until I told him the intensive happened primarily in a small group setting. Once he heard that, he was done. He said, "I would rather spend a weekend in the worst prison in America." I (Doug) have had similar responses. I invited a buddy to a Refreshing Your Marriage conference that I was speaking at in Southern California and he said, "Not if I have to sit in a circle and share stuff."

Coast to coast, the response is the same. For most men, the idea of sharing their feelings, or being called out for something they did wrong, is anything but appealing. This is why it is important for us to address their resistance in our promotion of small groups (and other marriage-related experiences, for that matter). They need to know that a small group gathering is not a support group or group therapy, where they'll be required to share their "issues."

> **We partnered with The Skit Guys to create a fun video that addresses men's fear. To preview it, go to http://marriedpeople.org/media/men-talking-to-men-about-small-groups-promotional-video.**

Another tip: Appeal to a man's ego, the part that longs to be on a winning team. Let him know that, in a small group, he will be surrounded by other leaders, other high quality men and women who are in a similar situation, and that he will have access to resources that will help his marriage win.

THE TIME FACTOR

Time isn't a sexist issue; both men and women are fearful of adding another commitment to their already full lives. We get it. We're the same way. It's normal in today's busy culture to ask yourself, "What's the reward?" before committing.

Good promotion needs to address all fears and obstacles, including time issues. One way to do that is to refer to these groups as an experiment: "We'd love for you to try a four- or six-week experiment where you get in a group with a few other couples like yourself." Consider giving groups an opportunity to "break up" after a certain trial time. Allow them to see that there's an "end clause" if it's not working. Even men think, *I can suffer through anything for four weeks.* Tell them that if this group is not the right fit, they can check out or try a different group.

Another idea is to offer a short-term commitment based on a topic: six weeks on sex (you'll have a crowd), five weeks on communication, that sort of thing. Essentially, you're enticing couples to try a group experience and appealing to those who aren't ready for a long-term commitment. As we've already stated, once they *taste* a genuinely caring small group, the rest is history—they'll feed themselves with this community.

SMALL GROUP OPTIONS

The great news is that most churches have small groups in one form or another. If that is true for your church, we suggest you integrate marriage curriculum in your existing small group structure. Whether you have an existing small group structure or not, here are a few relatively easy but effective ways to begin integrating small groups designed especially for married couples.

START ONE

Ask couples to give you five to eight weeks and you'll provide them with the materials to help them focus on their marriage. Again, don't be afraid to use the word *experiment* to calm their long-term commitment fears. These groups can meet anywhere: restaurants, on the church property, or in homes. The upside of meeting at the church is it relieves the discomfort of walking into a stranger's house. However, meeting in homes has several distinct advantages. It's more physically comfortable and inviting. It allows people to express their spiritual gift of hospitality. Plus, when people feel comfortable in a social setting, our experience has been that they tend to be more open relationally and theologically.

CHANGE ONE

At some point during the year, consider giving your existing small groups or Sunday school classes a break in their regular curriculum in order to focus on their marriage. You're not requesting that these groups become a "marriage" small group forever; you're simply encouraging them to change their focus for a short season. We realize some groups have been meeting so long they would rather die than change, and those groups may require a little special attention. (Or, you may choose to give those types no attention and spend your precious leadership time on those who are willing to change.)

HIGHLIGHT ONE

Every so often there may be a prime small group experience that you want everyone to have. When that happens, you will need to draw people's attention to it, highlight it in such a way that it really stands out. For instance, maybe you discover something designed not only for couples in crisis, but also for couples who want to make a good marriage great. (Who wouldn't want that "universal" kind of experience for the married people in their church?) Well, we've found some relevant materials that do just that.

In an effort to help struggling couples, we consulted with three professionals who specialize in helping troubled marriages: Shawn Stoever, Ph.D.; Terry Hargrave, Ph.D.; and Sharon Hargrave, MAMFC. Together, they have created an incredible small group resource called *5 Days to a New Marriage*.[21] The title and content comes from their wildly successful four- to five-day marriage intensives. Many couples show up to these intensives legally separated or with divorce papers in hand; most leave totally changed. Two years after the intensive, four out of five participating couples are **still together.**[22] However, this small group resource isn't just for couples whose marriages are foundering; it's for anyone who wants a stronger, healthier marriage.

We didn't think we could re-create a better wheel, so we partnered with these incredible thinkers. Their work is now part of the MarriedPeople Strategy. We encourage churches to offer their small groups the *5 Days to a New Marriage* material (which lasts 10 weeks). We continue to get positive feedback from users, including the fact that, once groups go through it, many couples get so much out of it that they want to step up and lead one the next time it's offered.

Which brings us to the next issue: finding good small group leaders.

RELUCTANT BUT WILLING

When hunting for small group leaders, we suggest you try to identify couples who fit the description "reluctant but willing." Many couples are *willing* to help because they have found hope in their own marriage and want to share it with others. That's nice, but a lot of people who want to *share* or *teach* don't have the servant heart that's needed to lead and shepherd a group of people. They're motivated by their own story, or by what they want to teach and convey to others, and sometimes that overconfidence leads to being overbearing. That's why it's wise to balance *willing* with *reluctant*. Being a little reluctant to lead a group because you don't feel like you have the "perfect" marriage is a good thing. A little apprehension can create a sincere dependence on God. These two factors can work well together.

Finding these types of couples requires you to do the difficult work on the front end through a vetting process. As any experienced leader knows, it's always easier to acquire a leader than fire one. So, make sure you establish some character qualities that you want for your small group leaders. Once you quantify the type of person you're looking for, it's a lot easier to qualify them for leading. (We'll talk a little more about finding and developing leaders in chapter 9.)

BETTER TOGETHER

Your church is probably filled with marriages like Jeremy and Tiffany Lees', with the potential to be radically altered through the influence of a **small group**[23] of committed, caring individuals. Think about what might happen to those couples in your church who are ready to call it quits—and will—unless someone gets close enough to say, "Oh no, that's not going to happen. You two are NOT getting divorced." Then they back up that radical statement with love and support.

The Bible is clear: we are better together, and when the church catches a vision for life-on-life relational ministry, powerful things can and will happen.

{ CHAPTER
SIX }

EQUIPPING

individual

COUPLES

{SIX}

THE TWO OF US

For several years, Woodmen Valley Chapel in Colorado Springs, Colorado, has offered regular "respite" events for families of children with special needs. Katie Garvert has led this ministry with the mindset that special needs ministry is a part of a holistic family ministry. As the special needs ministry grew, the church added the respite piece of programming. The purpose of the respite was not only to provide parents a break, but to provide spouses the opportunity to reconnect through time together alone.

But about a year ago Katie began noticing that mothers who once showed up at Respite check-in with their husbands were arriving without them. Instead of enjoying a date night, parents were doing their own thing, like running errands, while their children were in the church's care. As a mother herself, Katie recognized the value of a peaceful shopping trip, but was concerned that parents weren't refueling their marriage during this time. Katie also noticed that some of the parents who were spending this time together were showing up at pick-up more tense or sad, evidence that the "date" had not ended well.

Fresh off these observations, Katie felt burdened to work more proactively to help the marriage inside the family with special needs. Katie wanted to give these parents something that would keep them focused on each other, a tool that would facilitate constructive and encouraging conversation. Katie introduced couples to one of the components of the MarriedPeople Strategy we call Can't Wait Date Challenge.

As parents dropped off their children at Respite, they received a sheet of paper that had one of our Can't Wait Dates printed on it—step-by-step "date instructions" to go through together during their time without their kids. Katie said the response was amazing. Couples were refreshed, and their enthusiasm rejuvenated their whole approach to helping marriages. Parents were again going on dates (rather than running independent errands). And more importantly, both spouses were arriving at pick-up obviously having had a positive time together.

Katie said, "We realized that these parents had forgotten how to connect and were too tired and overwhelmed to plan a date for themselves. They didn't even know what to talk about aside from managing life details, usually related to the complex needs of their children. And many of these spouses had forgotten how to laugh. Among many things, the Date Night [Can't Wait Date] gave our couples fun conversation starters. And for the first time, husbands and wives were focused on each other. We saw this in their eyes and attitude when they arrived to pick up their children. I honestly had no idea that adding this simple tool would have such a huge impact on the families and on **our entire ministry.**"[24]

While it stands to reason that parents of children with special needs may carry a heavier burden than most parents (at least sometimes), all married couples know what it's like to be too busy, too stressed, and too serious. Every couple (in and outside the church) could benefit from connecting in new and creative ways, making memories that will enhance their marriages. Going out on a great date is just one way to do that.

OPTIONS FOR INDIVIDUAL COUPLE EXPERIENCES

As we've discussed, large groups have their benefits, and small groups are important, but there's something really powerful about **helping individual couples**.[25] However, as a ministry leader, you can't be on call 24/7 to meet every need of every married couple in your church. Each couple is different and therefore has unique needs; it would be impossible to meet all those needs yourself.

That's where this third on-ramp of the MarriedPeople Strategy (resources for individual couples) comes in. This is where we help you come alongside couples and support them in scalable ways—through date ideas, a monthly email, and personalized mentoring. Is there more that we could do? Sure. But these three opportunities are doable from a leadership standpoint and are practical in nature.

Here's the big picture: MarriedPeople Can't Wait Dates give couples an actual start-to-finish set of "instructions" for a fun, interactive date that they can easily accomplish on their own. The MarriedPeople E-ZINE (an email churches simply send out each month) offers couples encouragement and some laughs in a format that's easy to work into their day. MarriedPeople Down the Road helps churches set up opportunities for mentoring—that is, assisting those who are a little more seasoned in their marriage experience ("down the road" couples) to guide and encourage "mentee" couples in their unique needs. We'll unpack all three of these ideas to help you pull them off in your setting.

DATE NIGHTS

Date nights are a bright spot when it comes to what many churches are currently doing to help marriages. Twenty-seven of the 100 largest churches in the United States have sponsored a **date night at least once a year**.[26] The beauty of date nights from a leadership standpoint is that they meet a much-felt need, they're practical, and they require little to no budget. And date nights are another great way to shout to people in and around your church that you care about marriages.

WHY DATE NIGHTS?
Dates work

Our first date night initiative at North Point Community Church was called "The Great Date Experiment." Once a month for six months we rolled out a new great date. It truly was an experiment. We had no idea if couples would actually go out on the dates we were providing. But the response to the dates was overwhelming. North Point still creates Great Dates; they now call this effort the Great Date Experience because the experiment worked!

But helping couples date goes deeper than simply helping couples have a good time. The **National Marriage Project**,[27] located at the University of Virginia, concluded their study on date nights with the following comment: "Couples who devote time specifically to one another at least once a week are markedly more likely to enjoy high-quality relationships and lower divorce rates, compared to couples who do not devote much couple time to one another. If date nights are similarly valuable for couples, then the recent grassroots efforts to promote them around the nation may also foster higher-quality relationships and lower divorce rates in their sponsoring **communities**."[28]

Dates are what couples have asked for and what they best understand

We conducted a survey of couples in churches across the United States, and the most requested resource was **date ideas**.[29] Couples wanted "just add water"-type dates that they could easily do on their own. While there may be couples in your church who don't understand why they need to attend a larger group experience or participate in small groups, they *get* dating. Couples understand the *context* of dating (they used to do it); they simply struggle with *content*. The church can be the hero for marriages by giving people what they want and need. When we do, the response can be powerful. Jake and Elizabeth, married 28 years, wrote, "Tonight's date brought needed dialogue into our busy world. Our conversations focused on sweet memories and got us dreaming again. What a refreshing night. Thanks for doing all the work so we could just go out!"

Date nights help couples laugh

When people think about improving their marriage, their minds typically jump to words like *work; effort; long, intense conversations.* There's a reason for that; marriage is serious business. For most, *marriage* doesn't equate to *fun* and *laughter*. But we believe that, while some marriages are seriously ill (and therefore need serious help), laughter can provide some serious-enough medicine—and that a successful marriage strategy can serve up regular doses of it.

A cheerful heart is good medicine, but a crushed spirit dries up the bones. (Proverbs 17:22, NIV)

We also believe that a successful marriage strategy will help couples simply be together. Not every experience for individual couples needs to include an intense conversation reliving their latest issue or fight. We want couples to hang out, to enjoy time together. Many couples need help to do this, and that's why we created MarriedPeople Can't Wait Dates, instructions for dates specially designed so they can simply "add water" and go. After Blake and Rebecca went on one of these date nights, provided by their church, Rebecca said, "We had a blast. The funniest thing I learned was that he used to do push-ups before our dates so he would look buff … 21 years of marriage and I never knew."

Date nights help couples affirm each other

One of the easiest ways we can equip couples is to help them support each other. And one of the most straightforward ways to do that is to ask them questions likely to elicit affirmation. That's why, for example, every MarriedPeople Can't Wait Date includes a set of simple prompts like:

One of the nicest things you have ever done is _____.
Without you I would have never _____.
The thing I love about you most is _____.

(In fact, this is what triggered Blake and Rebecca's conversation—a simple question on their Can't Wait Date.) As odd as it sounds, we hear more positive feedback about these simple fill-in-the-blanks than almost anything we do. Why is this so powerful?

It's potent because for most couples, genuine encouragement is rare. Why do you think it's so rare? We're sure there are several answers, but where else in the world are men and women challenged to encourage their spouses?

As the church, we have that honor: to nudge couples gently to do something that they want and need, but may not do on their own.

Date nights help couples know each other

It's impossible to love someone on a consistent basis that you don't know. Timothy Keller, in his book *The Meaning of Marriage*, says:

> To be loved but not known is comforting but superficial. To be known and not loved is our greatest fear. But to be fully known and truly loved is, well, a lot like being loved by God. It is what we need more than anything. It liberates us from pretense, humbles us out of our self-righteousness, and fortifies us for any difficulty life can **throw at us.**[30]

Marriage expert **John Gottman**[31] has learned that healthy couples have a "love map," that place in the brain where you store all important information about **your spouse's life.**[32] When you remember your wife gets cold at the movies, you may grab a sweater in case she needs it—that's part of your love map. Your love map helps you remember your husband can't get enough chocolate, so you occasionally surprise him with a treat. These date night ideas are intended to facilitate some "mapping moments," unique opportunities that help couples continue to get to know each other in an easy, no-pressure, "this-is-not-therapy" kind of way. The shared time, and the things they learn about each other, equip couples to better love their spouse.

Date nights give couples relational wins

Few would argue that relationships can be confusing, really confusing. Maybe ambiguous is a better descriptor. It's often difficult to tell what our spouse is really thinking or feeling. It also can be hard to tell the true health of a relationship. By providing couples with step-by-step instructions for their dates (see graphic 6.1, below), you set them up to win by giving them something tangible. When couples experience a few relational wins, they may begin to believe they can make it. Ian and Becca, married four years, said it this way: "Thanks for re-centering me on how wonderful it truly is to be married to the person God brought me!"

Graphic 6.1

These wins make deposits into couples' relational accounts. In fact, these deposits become increasingly important memories for couples to draw upon when they're going through difficult challenges.

You may have a small percentage of couples who believe they don't need your effort and creativity when it comes to dating (and good for them). But you're more likely to have a larger number of couples who will thank you—we sure have.

HOW TO GET THE DATES INTO COUPLES' HANDS

Believe it or not, your biggest challenge to getting married couples to date isn't convincing them they need to date. Most married couples understand that quality time as a couple is important. Your biggest obstacle is getting them to pause their busy lives long enough to do it. How you distribute the dates greatly impacts participation. We have used several different methods for distributing our dates to couples. Here are the three that we found to be most effective. Trust yourself to choose the method that will work best for your church.

1. On-site pick up

Choose a date and a timeframe (e.g., Friday night from 5:00–7:00 p.m.) and ask couples to come to the church to pick up the date information. Meet them in the parking lot (don't make them get out of their cars) and give them a friendly greeting, a word of encouragement, and a printed copy of the date. It can simply be a sheet of paper with the date instructions (see graphic 6.1 above), or you can go more elaborate and present the date idea in a gift bag that includes coupons to restaurants, candy, and anything else fun you want to add.

Pros: Having a specific pick-up time requires a couple to plan ahead and be organized enough to get out of the house, increasing the likelihood that the date will actually happen. This option gives the couple a clear who, what, when, where, and how. You can also get accurate numbers of participants as well as their names in case you decide to follow up.

Cons: We don't really see much negative in this approach other than you (as the key leader) are standing outside or in another accessible place, waiting for people to show up. Obviously, this role could be delegated, but it's a fabulous opportunity for the leader of the marriage ministry to provide face-to-face encouragement. While it's not as convenient as the online method we'll describe below, it's definitely a winner.

Childcare: As we've previously mentioned, lack of childcare is a deal-killer for many couples. If you have the resources, you can provide childcare at your church property. You can also consider the childcare reimbursement method we mentioned in chapter 4. (See **Appendix 2**.)

2. Online download

Post the specific date idea on Facebook and your church website. Couples simply download the dates and participate at their convenience.

Pros: This is the most convenient method for many couples. This system also makes it easy for the date idea to go viral, allowing Joe Smith to send the date to his cousin in Brazil. A few date ideas created at North Point Community Church have been downloaded over 100,000 times in 58 different countries. (We think this Web-thing might be catching on.)

Cons: It's a little too convenient, passive, and easy to skip, triggering the "I'm tired—let's do it next weekend" excuse. As excited as we are about the viral potential, we've got to wonder how many times someone thought, *That's a good idea (we just downloaded); we'll do that when we have time.*

Childcare: Again, childcare is a big win. This particular method doesn't have a specific date attached to it, so it's difficult to plan childcare.

3. On-site pick up + online download combo

For this method, couples have a specific time to pick up the date (like option 1), but you also post it online a week or two later (option 2). If you choose this approach, we suggest you make the pick-up version of the date a little more elaborate. For instance, you can make a gift bag for each couple that contains date instructions; coupons to restaurants; a small group resource, a book, or candy; and so forth. Making a bigger deal of the pick up gives couples more incentive to choose option 1, which we believe increases the chances of them actually following through with the date.

Pros: This method combines the best of both options.

Cons: This can encourage procrastinators to further postpone if they know they have options other than a specific pick-up time.

Childcare: On-site childcare and childcare reimbursement works for this method as well.

4. Mobile apps

For this method you simply promote the available mobile date apps. MarriedPeople Can't Wait Dates, and other date night ideas, all exist on a mobile app platform called **gloo.**[33] **DateNightWorks. com**[34] also gives churches free date night programs.

Pros: The smart phone is a big part of life for many people— it's where they talk, text, schedule, and track relationships. Why not leverage it to empower marriages?

Cons: Believe it or not, some people still don't have or know how to use a smart phone.

A COUPLE OF COMMON COMMENTS ABOUT DATE NIGHTS

For some reason, providing date ideas for couples strikes some leaders as too simple to be powerful. But that's the beauty! There is power in its simplicity. Nonetheless, here are some of the common concerns we've consistently heard.

1. Isn't providing date nights for couples simply spoon-feeding them? Yes. That's exactly what it is. We believe providing dating ideas is similar to the spiritual milk that the Apostle Paul refers to in 1 Peter 2:2-3. Many marriages need some foundational ideas and help to get them growing. Once couples have tasted a great connection by going on an intentional date, they are more likely to develop an appetite for more. Those connections can help them grow as a couple and refresh and develop a dating habit. Obviously, our prayer is that these couples won't rely on our date night ideas forever, but will be inspired to create their own (and, who knows, maybe they'll become the couple who helps create date nights for others).

2. Date nights don't seem particularly spiritual. We hear this comment a lot at our seminars and do our best to communicate a compelling response by stating, "Divorce isn't 'spiritual' either." We believe that helping couples improve their marriage by taking small steps (like dating each other) is God-honoring. It's often a small, simple, helpful date idea, given freely, that leads couples through the front door of our MarriedPeople Strategy. When we ask small group participants or those who are being mentored how they got started with us, they usually reply that a free date night was the front door to their engagement and involvement.

Date night ideas aren't the only scalable way churches can support individual couples. There's the monthly MarriedPeople E-ZINE too.

MONTHLY EMAIL

On the 65-mile drive to my (Ted's) in-laws' house, we pass 29 churches. As we pass these churches, I usually wonder how many of them are intentional about helping marriages. Of the ones that are not, do they hold back because they believe they don't have the margin to pull off an effective strategy? Would they do something if they realized how simple and easy (and effective) it could be?

While we work hard to make the MarriedPeople Strategy as easy as possible, if only a tenth of those 29 churches said they couldn't do it, it would be worth our time and energy to create something they *could* do. That's why our team created the **MarriedPeople E-ZINE**.[35] The E-ZINE is a man-friendly monthly email churches simply forward to the married people in their church. Sure, churches may have to collect a few email addresses and get a high school student to push a few buttons, but this is still easy, breezy stuff. And not only have we made it easy for church leaders, we have made it even easier for the married people who will read it each month.

The email is designed to encourage couples and give them some laughs as they enjoy the different bite-size segments:

- He Said, She Said—Each month, we highlight a couple we think has something great to say. We give them one question to ask each other and provide their answer here.

- Hot Button—Each month, we ask a Christian therapist to share one simple thing that could dramatically impact marriages.
- Random Awesomeness—One or two websites to check out simply because they're funny, amazing, cool . . . you get the idea.
- Post It—A specific, encouraging fill-in-the-blank for couples to write and post to each other on a sticky note.
- The Spice—One tip designed to bring couples closer in the bedroom.
- 2-minute Vacation—One out-of-the-ordinary question couples can ask each other.
- Plugged In—Each month, we explore a different way to get healthier, spiritually, physically, mentally, and emotionally.

You may be thinking, *Isn't this more spoon-feeding? It doesn't seem to require a lot of the reader.* Again, if that's what you are thinking, then yes, you're right. But dream with us a bit:

- Imagine a typical married couple encouraging another couple not to make "small deals" into "big deals."
- Imagine a couple learning from a counselor without entering his or her office.
- Imagine a couple laughing together at a silly YouTube video on a day that has been tough otherwise.
- Imagine a wife (or husband) lifting the washing machine lid for the millionth time and discovering a Post-it Note that reads, "Thank you for washing so many loads of clothes. It is very much appreciated! I love you!"

- Imagine a couple understanding for the first time that they are wired differently sexually, and learning a new way to play that to their advantage.
- Imagine a couple spending a few minutes dreaming about an amazing vacation.
- Imagine a couple praying for each other, maybe for the first time.

Imagine. If **10 minutes a day of meaningful conversation**[36] can help a couple have a longer, healthier marriage, isn't it possible for them to thrive with a few intentional and engaging prompts? We think so.

While the E-ZINE is a resource designed especially for churches that can't do anything else, it's an effective tool for any church because it gives couples bite-size wins without overwhelming them with content.

Another effective (and scalable) tool in any church's toolbox is mentoring.

MENTORING

I (Ted) had the privilege of watching my son be baptized at an event our church calls "Family Birthday Celebration." It was an amazing program from start to finish. The music, the speaker, the food, the decorations, each child's story of faith on video—really, everything was done with excellence. But without a doubt, the most powerful and touching element was experiencing the event with my son's small group leaders—Josh and Gabe—two tenth-grade boys who love Jesus and my 10-year-old son.

My son (Judson) loves Josh and Gabe; my wife and I do too, for their influence on our son. These guys not only show up on

Sunday mornings to lead Judson's small group, they show up in his "real" world too, like his Saturday football games. Every Sunday when we go to his church classroom to pick him up, we go through the same routine: they've hidden Judson somewhere in the room and tell us (loud enough for our son to hear), "We don't know where he is." As odd as this sounds, that particular moment (which is such a small thing) is one of Judson's favorite moments of the week. Are you getting the picture?

Now back to the Family Birthday Celebration: our hearts were full as the boys stood with us to watch our son get baptized. Then it hit me—why does the mentoring relationship have to stop when children graduate from high school? That's where it stops for many kids. But, biblically speaking, it shouldn't. The Apostle Paul painted a broader picture of walking in the ways of Jesus when he wrote, **"Follow my example, as I follow the example of Christ." (1 Corinthians 11:1, NIV)** And, **"Whatever you have learned or received or heard from me, or seen in me—put it into practice." (Philippians 4:9, NIV)**

/////

Leaders, think how powerful it would be if every marriage experienced what Judson experienced. This is not only true for pre-marital and newlywed couples; we believe a caring and committed couple to mentor *every* couple could be revolutionary. Regardless of how long people have been married, regardless if they are struggling, simply surviving, or growing in their marriage, every couple could benefit from a more experienced (older) couple cheering them on. This is not an unrealistic dream. To address this issue, we created MarriedPeople Down the Road.

MARRIEDPEOPLE DOWN THE ROAD

We intentionally chose not to use the word *mentor* in the title because it can be too intimidating for potential mentors *and* mentees. Instead of using this term that, for some, is loaded with too much expectation and fear, we simply suggest that every couple needs another couple who is a little "farther down the (marriage) road." These "down the road" couples don't need to be perfect; but they do need to have a love for Jesus and a healthy, growing marriage. They also need to be willing to meet occasionally with the other couple; be willing to listen; be (appropriately) transparent about their own marriage; and be willing to journey with, support, and cheer that couple on.

Our process of connecting a couple to a couple starts, continues, and ends with questions:

Step One: Ask potential MarriedPeople Down the Road couples to fill out a questionnaire. (See **Appendix 3**, "MarriedPeople Down the Road [Leader] Questionnaire.")

Step Two: Ask the couples who are looking for a Down the Road (mentor) couple to fill out a questionnaire too. (See **Appendix 4**, "MarriedPeople Down the Road Questionnaire.")

Step Three: Use the questionnaires to help you match couples. Matching couples up with one another is not a science, but there should be some answers on the questionnaire that make you think, *They might be a good fit with the Johnsons.*

Step Four: Ask the newly matched-up couples to experiment with this new relationship by sharing "just a meal." Over a meal, the mentors and mentees discuss the questions and answers from their questionnaires. At the end of the meal, if both couples feel like they're a fit, then the mentor-mentee relationship begins and they move to Step Five. If not, no problem; it was *just a meal*. Hopefully, it's only a matter of time before pairing them with another couple.

Step Five: We suggest the couples meet at least one time a month for six months. Once a month we suggest the mentor couple do three things: Connect with their mentee couple with a text or an email; have a meal or coffee with their mentee couple; and suggest a particular resource or book to their mentee couple.

This schedule is by no means written in stone. At the same time, people want to know what's expected of them. So we suggest you give Down the Road couples very clear guidelines of how and when you expect them to meet with mentee couples. You can create your own list of expectations for your Down the Road couples, but here's one to get you started.

TEN EXPECTATIONS FOR COUPLES DOWN THE ROAD

1. Determine with your mentee couple a set time to meet, and attend all meeting times.
2. Connect with your mentee couple outside of your set meeting times (via text, email, or phone) at least once a week.
3. Offer tools and resources to couples you think will be helpful.
4. Determine with your mentee couple what you hope to accomplish.

5. Keep what your mentee couple shares in strictest confidence.

6. Listen, listen, listen.

7. Don't feel like you have to have all the answers. Simply share what you have learned from your experience.

8. Hold mentee couples accountable to their goals.

9. Give tangible ways couples can achieve their goals.

10. Ask mentee couples how you can serve them better.

11. Celebrate when mentee couples make steps toward their goals.

DO INDIVIDUAL COUPLE EXPERIENCES REALLY MAKE A DIFFERENCE?

For most Christian parents, there are few things more rewarding than catching your children making Jesus-connections on their own: You walk into your son's room and see his Bible flopped open on the bed. Your daughter's small group leader reports that she's the only one in the group who shows empathy for that one awkward kid in the group. At dinner, your son prays in a tone that is natural and genuinely grateful. It's such a gift, as a parent, to see a child's faith finally become his or her own.

As leaders who focus on marriage, we experience a similar feeling when we see couples focused on their own marriages. It does our hearts good to see responsibility and movement toward marital health. For example:

- You see a couple (who hasn't dated since their child was born seven years ago) going on the dates that you've provided.

- A mentor couple tells you one of their mentee couples had a huge relational breakthrough once they realized why they were fighting.
- An empty-nest couple volunteers to mentor because their own mentors made such a difference in their marriage.

It's rewarding to see couples, on their own, finally giving their marriage the priority it deserves. Just as any caring parents want to help their children develop habits that build their own faith, we want to help married people develop healthy habits that will enhance their faith and deepen their marriage.

ESCAPE

from

CONTENT

MOUNTAIN

{SEVEN}

HOW MUCH IS TOO MUCH?

How would you explain how to walk to someone?

How about: "Walking (also known as ambulation) is one of the main gaits of locomotion among legged animals, and is typically slower than running and other gaits ... Human walking is accomplished with a strategy called the double pendulum. During forward motion, the leg that leaves the ground swings forward from the hip. This sweep is the first pendulum. Then the leg strikes the ground with the heel and rolls through to the toe in a motion described as an inverted pendulum. The motion of the two legs is coordinated so that one foot or the other is always in contact with the ground. The process of walking recovers approximately sixty per cent of the energy used due to pendulum dynamics and **ground reaction force**."[37]

It's not unusual for those of us committed to helping marriages to sound like this (the example above). We're notorious for overexplaining; we give people too much background or clinical reasons for why relationships do or don't work. Granted, sometimes that approach is necessary. But most of the time it's not. Most marriages need the simplicity of "just take one step" instead of long, laborious expositions about "ambulation."

That's why we designed the MarriedPeople Strategy to be (1) consistent; (2) encouraging; and (3) simple (i.e., "I can do that!"). We want couples to "just take one step," to take that one step often, and to know that you're cheering them on as they do.

Below are some of the guidelines we use to create content and programming. We believe they will help you as you consider moving forward in your marriage strategy.

TEACH LESS FOR MORE

Through the years, we've learned from others much wiser than ourselves that …

If you teach people less, they will actually learn more.

At first, this principle may feel counter-intuitive. It may raise questions because it's a principle that's rarely applied, especially within ministry to married couples.

However, for most marriages, more content is not better. Leaders who favor "more is more" seem to believe if we give people enough information, *some*thing is certain to work. So (according to this mindset), the more stats and data and principles and steps we throw at them, the better off they'll be. Here's the problem we've observed with this line of thinking: people who are married often feel overwhelmed by what they should be doing but aren't. Heaping more content on them can become the tipping point between "energized and encouraged" and "giving up."

We ache at the thought of a husband or a wife who is struggling in marriage trying to navigate the plethora of resources available to them. They're already running low on emotional energy as they approach the marriage section in a bookstore (Christian or secular) and try to discern which of the many, many books will be most helpful. Which author is right? Who should they steer away from? There's no question there's helpful material within many of those books; the problem for the average Joe and Sue is that they don't have a clue about how to select the "right" book. And if they retreat from their experience at the bricks-and-mortar store to online resources, they're inundated with even more complexity and confusion.

Unfortunately, churches often take a similar approach. They schedule a weekend marriage retreat, for instance, that requires thirsty couples to drink from a fire hose, or tired couples to hike to the highest mountain to get the richest content. Or they plan a five-week sermon series on marriage, giving couples enough content to last them for several years until they do a series again. These well-intentioned church leaders offer couples everything they know about marriage, and arguably, it's great content. But it's simply too much.

In and outside the church, when it comes to helping marriages, it seems we are content heavy and application light. What's the answer to this dilemma? Simple. Teach less for more.

Here are two specific ways to put this principle into practice:

Give Couples Less Content More Often

Instead of covering a lot of ground at a retreat or through a sermon series, narrow your focus to only the most important topics (more on that next) and talk about them more often. Whatever marriage-supportive experiences your church offers (larger group events, small groups, individual couple experiences, or some combination of these), give people the opportunity to take "just one step" weekly, biweekly, or monthly. If you can't do anything else, give couples a step-by-step date opportunity once a quarter and send them the MarriedPeople E-ZINE monthly email resource. These simple, bite-size resources help couples succeed in practical ways.

Move from General to Focused

While there are many effective marriage principles and practices, giving couples a single, clear, focused message is powerful. Simply reduce the total number of topics you *could* cover to just a few essentials, or key values, that you will cover. Perhaps the most successful example of this in the marriage space is Gary Chapman's The *5 Love Languages*. Millions have connected to these five relatively simple ideas and use his nomenclature (including us; see the example in the next section about words of affirmation).

Similarly, the MarriedPeople Strategy uses a clear, consistent vocabulary throughout, but just as important, it condenses a multitude of principles and practices into a few key values—four, to be exact, derived from the precious few verses on marriage that Scripture offers. We refer to these as …

The Core 4 Habits of a Great Marriage

Graphic 7.1

1. **Have serious fun.** Having fun as a couple is not optional; it's essential to a healthy marriage. We believe the best way to protect your marriage is to enjoy it regularly.

2. **Respect and love.** Of the few verses God directs toward husbands and wives, we are told more often to respect and love each other than anything else. This truth really can set us free when we understand the interplay of respect and love.

3. **Love God first.** When Jesus was asked about the greatest commandment, His answer was to love God with all you are and to love others as well as you love yourself. Loving God in your "individual" life greatly impacts your married life.

4. **Practice your promise.** Our spouses trusted that we would do what we promised when we said "I do"—to love each other and to stay together no matter what. Knowing and experiencing a lasting commitment is vital to every marriage.

See **Appendix 5** for a more detailed explanation of the Core 4 Habits as well as its scriptural foundation.

A second guideline that shapes the design of the MarriedPeople Strategy is . . .

PROVIDE "GO AND DO'S" SO THEY WILL GO AND DO

Would you rather married people spend an hour reading a chapter in a marriage book on the importance of affirming their spouse, or have them spend 10 minutes (as part of their date night) filling in the following blanks for each other?

1. I am impressed with how much you know about _____.
2. Something special about you that not many people see is _____.
3. One of the nicest things you've ever done is _____.

When we "tested" these questions on a date night with our wives, it was powerful—so powerful we couldn't stop talking about it afterward. We both agreed that we could live happily for months on the impact of the words our wives spoke to us on that trial date. (Both of us share the same primary love language, à la Gary Chapman: words of affirmation.) We knew this was going to work, and we've been right.

Why does it work? Marriages need simple wins. When we give couples small, clear, tangible actions to take that will improve their marriage, those wins—even though they're small—can become life changing. And the more practical, the better. We certainly found this to be true with our blog titles. For instance, my (Ted) post "3 One-Liners that Made a Difference in Our Marriage" was far more popular than another of my posts, "A Different Way of

Looking at Things." Why? Because the first is practical, the second is philosophical. Marketing-types understand this principle and implement it by creating book and seminar titles that offer hope. Next time you see a magazine rack, peruse the covers; you'll see the hope they're trying to deliver: *5 Ways to . . . 4 Tricks to a Better . . . 3 Simple Actions to Improve Your . . . 1 Step Every Successful Person Must Take . . .*

So, when in doubt, give couples something you know they can and will do. In fact, if I (Ted) could go back and do one thing differently in the first few years I served married couples, I would have made our go and do's much more go and doable.

FAQs REGARDING THE MARRIEDPEOPLE CORE 4

1. Do we have to use the Core 4 Habits? Absolutely not. Use whatever you want. You're more than welcome to "borrow" our four habits or to make up your own. We have no illusions that we've cornered the market on the core values every marriage ministry should embrace. Actually, it's one of the mini-battles that we (Doug and Ted) commonly have when we talk MarriedPeople Strategy. Doug thinks there should be a few more and Ted thinks there should be four. What matters most is that you choose some key values and keep a consistent language so the "slow-learning, slow-adopter" couples will eventually catch on to what you're trying to do with them. Furthermore, in chapter 10 we'll give you step-by-step instructions for how you might implement your own key values.

2. Is there a particular order to the Core 4? Yes and no. You can put them in any order you like, but we recommend that you stay consistent. If you choose to use our resources and strategy, we recommend you use them in this order:

- Have Serious Fun
- Respect and Love
- Love God First
- Practice Your Promise

We placed them in this order because we've found that starting off on a fun note is helpful when it comes to reaching males. "Having Serious Fun" is not more important than "Loving God First," but we think guys will tend to find it easier to love God once they've experienced a safe element of fun. We wanted "Practice Your Promise" to be the last of the four because it lends itself to moments of commitment—which is a strong way to finish the year. At the same time, other churches have found success using them in a different order. As always, feel free to change any of our ideas to fit your context.

3. Will people get tired of the Core 4? Not if you are intentional. Although we would caution you about the "graduation mentality." Whatever language you choose to use as part of your marriage strategy (the Big 3, the Core 4, the Sexy 6, whatever), make it clear to couples that they will hear these terms over and over. When you first present the Core 4 Habits (or whatever language you choose), some people may assume they will hear about each Habit once— and that that will be sufficient. They'll be tempted to approach all marriage events or experiences from a checklist perspective. If you use one of the Habits as part of your promo (e.g., "This Friday night we'll be focusing on 'Have Serious Fun' "), you may discover people

SMALL GROUP EXPERIENCES: VININGS LAKE

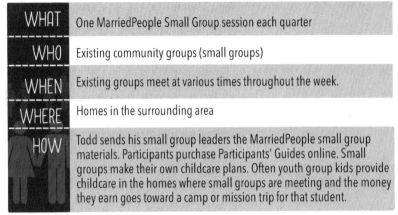

WHAT	One MarriedPeople Small Group session each quarter
WHO	Existing community groups (small groups)
WHEN	Existing groups meet at various times throughout the week.
WHERE	Homes in the surrounding area
HOW	Todd sends his small group leaders the MarriedPeople small group materials. Participants purchase Participants' Guides online. Small groups make their own childcare plans. Often youth group kids provide childcare in the homes where small groups are meeting and the money they earn goes toward a camp or mission trip for that student.

Graphic 11.16

INDIVIDUAL COUPLES EXPERIENCES: VININGS LAKE

	DATE NIGHTS	MARRIEDPEOPLE E-ZINE EMAILS
WHAT	Date Night PDFs	MarriedPeople E-ZINE Email (Monthly email with insights and suggestions)
WHO	All couples	All couples in church email database
WHEN	Quarterly	First Monday of every month
WHERE	Date Night instructions are picked up as couples leave church on Sunday mornings.	Church forwards to married couples in the church database
HOW	Couples receive a sealed envelope containing the Date Night. Church doesn't provide childcare.	

Graphic 11.17

VININGS LAKE CALENDAR

	FIRST QUARTER		
	JANUARY	**FEBRUARY**	**MARCH**
	Larger Group Experience	Small Group Session	Date Night PDF Posted
	5 Days to a New Marriage Small Groups for couples who are struggling.	MarriedPeople E-ZINE	MarriedPeople E-ZINE
	MarriedPeople E-ZINE		

	SECOND QUARTER		
	APRIL	**MAY**	**JUNE**
	Larger Group Experience	Small Group Session	Date Night PDF Posted
	MarriedPeople E-ZINE	MarriedPeople E-ZINE	MarriedPeople E-ZINE

	THIRD QUARTER		
	JULY	**AUGUST**	**SEPTEMBER**
	Larger Group Experience	Small Group Session	*5 Days to a New Marriage* Small Groups for couples who are struggling.
	MarriedPeople E-ZINE	MarriedPeople E-ZINE	Date Night PDF Posted
			MarriedPeople E-ZINE

	FOURTH QUARTER		
	OCTOBER	**NOVEMBER**	**DECEMBER**
	Larger Group Experience	Small Group Session	Date Night PDF Posted
	MarriedPeople E-ZINE	MarriedPeople E-ZINE	MarriedPeople E-ZINE

Graphics 11.18 - 11.21

Leadership Encouragement: When we asked Todd what he would want to say to you, he said, "Just do it! Marriages need you. All marriages need you. The entire MarriedPeople Strategy has already done the difficult part for you! All you have to do is get it on the calendar and start fostering healthy marriages within your church community. If I can do it, anyone can."

NO ONE WAY

We chose to highlight just a few of the churches that have embraced the MarriedPeople Strategy so you could better see the variety of ways it is implemented. There is no one way to do everything we've suggested. There are many ways to help marriages, and whether you use the MarriedPeople Strategy or something else, we'd challenge you to be clear. If your strategy is confusing, the couples in your church won't be able to explain it easily. Your best marketing will come word-of-mouth from changed lives. Remember: when in doubt, choose clear.

BEFORE
you
GO

DREAM WITH US

Let's return to Blake, Beth, Sara, and Jenny, the family we described at the beginning of the book. Make no mistake about it: Blake, Beth, Sara, and Jenny live in your neighborhood and go to your church. Whether you believe in 2 percent or 90 percent of what we have written, this family needs you. But if you are a church leader, we know it would be easy to put this book on the shelf and move on with life and ministry. After all, Sunday is coming and marriage can wait. Or can it? Married couples need the church now, despite the fact you will probably never read real headlines like these:

**Local Family of Five Splits Forever, Leaving
Children to Make Sense of It**

**Couple's Tension Escalates to Point
Where Home Is Unbearable**

**18-year-old Vows Never to Marry to Avoid Pain
She Associates with Marriage**

What would be the headlines no one will ever read about the marriages surrounding your church? Who is speaking up for those children? Who is coming to the rescue of those families? The church can play a huge role in rescuing marriages from divorce and mediocrity.

FIRST RESPONDERS

When natural disasters hit an area, it often brings out the best in people. Everyday people become heroes simply because their hearts break.

At the risk of sounding dramatic, there is a marital disaster sweeping through every community. It's time for the church to lead the charge against it. It's time for the church to make first responders out of everyday people by equipping them to address marriages at every level, from struggling to surviving to growing. As we do, the amazing stories of rescue, and the not-so-amazing stories of prevention, will not make the news either. You won't read the following headlines:

**Wife and Mother Decides to Give It One More Try with
Her Husband After Attending a Marriage Event at Church**

**Couple Burns Divorce Papers After Finding Hope,
Healing for Their Marriage in Small Group**

**Church Helps Tired, Overworked Couple Date
Their Way Back to Wholeness**

Even so, is it still worth the effort? The children would say yes. The couples would say yes. You would say yes. We would say yes. We passionately believe ministry to married couples can no longer wait. The time is now. We believe the time is right for the local church to take marriage "in house." That really is the distinction to what we are suggesting. But because we know that most church staffs are overcommitted as it is, we want to do everything possible to make taking marriage "in house" as fun, easy, powerful, and relevant as possible.

That's why we wrote this book and why we created MarriedPeople. We've got a long way to go, but this is what we are seeing more and more every day: church leaders are bringing marriage "in house," with effects that are nothing short of miraculous.

You can do this. Your church can do this. God isn't looking for married people with perfect marriages to start the ministry to married couples at your church. He's looking for a faithful few, those who are willing to trust Him to do what only He can do. Is that you? Is that someone you know? Either way, we pray you at least start the process toward your church helping marriages.

On behalf on the Blakes, Beths, Saras, and Jennys in your church and community, please take one step toward empowering your church to build marriages that last. We encourage you to pause right now for 30 seconds and pray just one simple prayer: "God, what would You have our church do to help marriages?"

Please let us know your story, questions, and prayers at **facebook.com/marriedpeople**.

APPENDICES

APPENDIX 1

10 QUESTIONS TO CONSIDER AS YOU PREPARE
YOUR MESSAGE

It's easy for hosts and speakers at larger group experiences to forget to address everyone in the audience. As you determine your host script and the content of your message, we suggest you always ask the following questions:

1. Am I giving those who are struggling some hope?
2. Am I giving those who are simply surviving in their marriage some compelling vision to improve?
3. Am I giving those who have a strong marriage an opportunity to serve others?
4. Am I speaking to all life stages and common situations: newly married, first-time parents, empty nesters, and blended families?
5. Am I communicating that I don't live in the clouds and I understand the pressures and realities of their world?
6. Am I being (appropriately) transparent, opening up some issues and struggles in my own marriage?
7. Am I sharing from my own experience that I know what it's like to find hope in my marriage?
8. Will women feel like they were represented?
9. Will men feel respected?
10. Ultimately, at the end of the night, did I point people back to Jesus?

APPENDIX 2

SAMPLE CHILDCARE REIMBURSEMENT FORM

CHILDCARE REIMBURSEMENT

Name*

Address*

Email Address

Group Leader or Event*

Event Date*

Number of Children*

Number of Hours*

Amount*

*Required field

CHILDCARE REIMBURSEMENT RATES

	1 HOUR	1.5 HOURS	2 HOURS	2.5 HOURS	3 HOURS
1 CHILD	$7.00	$10.50	$14.00	$17.50	$21.00
2 CHILDREN	$7.50	$11.25	$15.00	$18.75	$22.50
3 CHILDREN	$8.00	$12.00	$16.00	$20.00	$24.00
4 CHILDREN	$8.50	$12.75	$17.00	$21.25	$25.50

Childcare for more than 4 children will be reimbursed at $9.00 per hour.

Instructions for processing your childcare reimbursement request:
1. Please complete the form above, including your name and address, Small Group Leader's name, date of meeting, number of children, number of hours, and amount requested (based on the chart above).
2. For accounting purposes, please submit request no later than 30 days after event.
3. Use chart above to figure amounts due. You must submit one form per event.
4. You can expect reimbursement check within 2 to 3 weeks from date of submission.

APPENDIX 3

MARRIEDPEOPLE DOWN THE ROAD
(LEADER) QUESTIONNAIRE

---

1. How long have you been married?

2. Do you have any children? If so, how many and what are their ages?

3. What is your greatest strength as a couple?

4. What is your greatest challenge as a couple?

5. Why do you want to be a married couple "down the road"?

APPENDIX 4

MARRIEDPEOPLE DOWN THE ROAD QUESTIONNAIRE

1. How long have you been married?

2. Do you have any children? If so, how many and what are their ages?

3. What is your greatest strength as a couple?

4. What is your greatest challenge as a couple?

5. Which of the following best describes your marriage?
   - Struggling
   - Surviving
   - Growing

6. What do you hope to gain by meeting with a married couple who is "down the road"?

APPENDIX 5

CORE 4 HABITS

Core Habit: Have Serious Fun

This seemingly light-hearted Habit comes from a serious passage, Proverbs 5.

For 14 verses, Solomon warns his son against adultery. He warns him about the woman whose lips "drip honey," whose speech is "smoother than oil," whose "steps lead straight to the grave." After a list of don'ts, he gets to the do's beginning with verse 15:

> **Drink water from your own cistern,**
> **running water from your own well.**
> **Should your springs overflow in the streets,**
> **your streams of water in the public squares?**
> **Let them be yours alone,**
> **never to be shared with strangers.**
> **May your fountain be blessed,**
> **and may you rejoice in the wife of your youth.**
> **A loving doe, a graceful deer—**
> **may her breasts satisfy you always,**
> **may you ever be intoxicated with her love.**
> **(Proverbs 5:15-19, NIV)**

Notice how these "do" verses are filled with feeling words such as *rejoice, satisfied,* and *intoxicated.* However, Solomon is not directing his son to *feel* something, but to *focus* on someone—the wife God gave him. He is saying to his son, and to all married people, "It's great you want to have sex; simply have it with the one God gave you." By having consistent, passionate sex with our spouses, we protect ourselves and our spouses from what happens when we attempt to satisfy that appetite with someone or something other than our spouses. Sexual intimacy with our spouses not only protects us from the one that "leads us straight to the grave," it provides us with an incredible connection to our spouses. Sex is not extra for married couples; it's essential.

These verses not only allude to the amazing connection that's possible through sexual intimacy, they get at a relational connection that can only be experienced by married people. Matthew Henry puts it this way, "It is not only allowed us, but commanded us, to be pleasant with our relations; and it particularly becomes yoke-fellows to rejoice together and in each other." Henry goes on to say—and don't miss this—"Mutual delight is the bond of mutual fidelity."*

These verses are powerful because they don't paint a picture of married couples simply surviving or being committed to not getting a divorce, but a picture of two people who are rejoicing, satisfied, and intoxicated. As the church, we have the privilege of spreading that good news.

We took the do's in these verses and put them under one Habit, Have Serious Fun:

- "Have," because it's a choice.
- "Serious," because this most intimate connection between husband and wife (that includes sex, delight, and joy) is not something to be taken lightly; it's seriously important.
- "Fun," because it's a modern term that sums up delight, fondness, rejoicing, joy, and (euphemistically) sex.

Bottom line: We believe having fun as a couple is not just something extra. It's essential. In fact, we believe the best way to protect your marriage is to enjoy it.

Core Habit: Respect and Love

The following verses have often been considered the most important biblical mandate for marriage. They have also been some of the most controversial.

Submit to one another out of reverence for Christ.

Wives, submit yourselves to your own husbands as you do to the Lord. For the husband is the head of the wife as Christ is the head of the church, his body, of which he is the Savior. Now as the church submits to Christ, so also wives should submit to their husbands in everything.

Husbands, love your wives, just as Christ loved the church and gave himself up for her to make her holy, cleansing her by the washing with water through the word, and to present her to himself as a radiant church, without stain or wrinkle or any other blemish, but holy and blameless. In this same way, husbands ought to love their wives as their own bodies. He who loves his wife loves himself. After all, no one ever hated their own body, but they feed and care for their body, just as Christ does the church—for we are members of his body. "For this reason a man will leave his father and mother and be united to his wife, and the two will become one flesh." This is a profound mystery—but I am talking about Christ and the church. However, each one of you also must love his wife

as he loves himself, and the wife must respect her husband. (Ephesians 5:21-33, NIV)

These verses are a point of contention for many, especially women, and understandably so. After all, most of us have heard of unconditional love. In fact, you don't have to be a Christian to appreciate a man who loves his wife unconditionally. Reading in the Bible that a husband "must love his wife" just feels right, even heroic. But we can see why some people push back when they are told a wife "must respect her husband." Dr. Emerson Eggerichs writes in his best-selling book, *Love & Respect*, "Time and again I've had women tell me they've never heard the two words *unconditional respect* put together in the context of a relationship. For them, it is literally an oxymoron."† But as any man will tell you, unconditional respect is just as powerful to a man as unconditional love is to a woman—heroic, even. The purpose of this passage isn't so much about defining roles, or establishing a hierarchy, as it is about revealing the greatest desire of men and the greatest desire of women: men greatly desire to be unconditionally respected, and women greatly desire to be unconditionally loved.

Current research underscores the same. Secular therapists and authors Patricia Love, Ed.D., and Steven Stosny, Ph.D., report that research has overwhelmingly proven that men have a heightened sensitivity to shame and inadequacy, while women have a heightened sensitivity to the fear of being isolated and shut out. They have discovered that much of the tension married couples experience is a result of the connection between fear and shame: when a woman feels shut out by her husband, she shames him; when a man feels shamed by his wife, he shuts down; which makes her fearful; which then leads to her shaming him; which makes him fearful … you get the cycle.‡ Now imagine helping the couples of your church to swap shame for unconditional respect and fear for unconditional love. That's powerful stuff.

Bottom line: While men need love from their wives, and wives need respect from their husbands, the primary desire of a man is to be unconditionally respected while the primary desire of woman is to be unconditionally loved.

Core Habit: Love God First

When someone asked Jesus which of the commandments was most important, He had a quick and clear answer.

> **Jesus replied: "'Love the Lord your God with all your heart and with all your soul and with all your mind.' This is the first and greatest commandment. And the second is like it: 'Love your neighbor as yourself.' All the Law and the Prophets hang on these two commandments."**
> **(Matthew 22:37-40, NIV)**

Jesus makes it abundantly clear where we are to direct our hearts, souls, and minds first: toward God. Secondly, we are to love our neighbor—which of course includes our spouses. What could be more impactful in today's culture, in which too many people look at marriage as a relationship whose primary purpose is to meet their needs? Tom Cruise's character in the movie *Jerry Maguire* goes so far as to say that a spouse is supposed to "complete me." Sounds romantic, but it's bad theology. God is the only one capable of completing us.

But loving God "first" is also one of the most important things (if not *the* most important thing) we can do for our marriages.

Because what happens when we love God first, when we abide by the Spirit? It changes who we are. It changes not only how we love God; it changes how we love each other. Galatians 5 says we bear fruit through our relationship with God: love, joy, peace, patience, kindness, goodness, faithfulness, gentleness, and self-control. Now, imagine your spouse using those words to describe you. Imagine the married people in your church using those words to describe their spouses.

But do you have to love God *first* in order to love your spouse *well*? We have all seen the exceptions. Maybe you have neighbors, friends, or family members who are not believers but have what you would call a very loving marriage. Most of us have also seen marriages that were lousy or that end in divorce despite the fact that both spouses loved God. Any time you are dealing with two people, there are no absolutes. But there is absolutely nothing you can do to love your spouse more than loving God with all your heart. For most of us, it postures us to love them in a way we could never love them on our own.

Bottom line: Developing a love affair with God will greatly impact one's married life. That's why this Core Habit is so important to repeat, over and over.

Core Habit: Practice Your Promise
May you rejoice in the wife of your youth.
(Proverbs 5:18b, NIV)

Be on your guard, and do not be unfaithful to the wife of your youth. (Malachi 2:15d, NIV)

Why the reference to the "wife of your youth"? The intent was to remind each spouse of the day when he or she "stood at the altar" and made a covenant in front of God, family, and friends that he or she would be faithful until death. When these passages were written, a covenantal relationship was a big deal. Often a simple reminder of the covenant was all that was necessary to draw the couple toward obedience. But the covenant wasn't just about the "big day"; it was what the covenant promised on the big day that they needed to do every day.

Bottom line: We made a big promise when we said "I do." Our spouses trusted that we would do what we promised to do: to love each other and to stay together no matter what. Making—and being able to rely on—that commitment is absolutely essential to every marriage.

*See *Matthew Henry's Commentary on the Whole Bible*. You can find it online at sites like http://www.biblestudytools.com/commentaries/matthew-henry-complete/proverbs/5.html.

†Emerson Eggerichs, *Love & Respect: The Love She Most Desires, the Respect He Desperately Needs* (Nashville: Thomas Nelson, Inc., 2004), 43. Kindle edition.

‡Patricia Love and Steven Stosny, *How to Improve Your Marriage Without Talking About It* (New York: Broadway Books, 2007). Kindle edition.

APPENDIX 6

TOPICAL INDEX

People often ask us where different "hot topics" fit under the Core 4 Habits. The way you organize topics is completely up to you, but we thought this topical index might assist you.

Have Serious Fun
- Sex
- Dating
- Romance

Respect and Love
- Communication
- Differences
- Priorities

Love God First
- Finances
- In-laws
- Children/teenagers
- Praying as a couple
- Devotions as a couple

Practice Your Promise
- Commitment
- Marriage milestones
- Avoiding divorce
- Mentoring
- Pre-marital

APPENDIX 7

LEADERS MEETING AGENDA

1. Show Vision Video. (Go to http://marriedpeople.org/media/vision-video.)

2. Welcome

3. Show two-minute Strategy Video. (Go to http://player.vimeo.com/video/64035603?autoplay=1.)

4. Discuss the Seven Shifts. (See chapter 3 in this book.)

5. Show diagram of the three MarriedPeople experiences. (See graphic 3.1, chapter 3.)

6. Express how this ministry ties into the overall vision of the church. (See step one, in "Understand your pastor's position," chapter 9.)

7. Share your personal marriage story.

8. Cast vision: What would happen if we were able to keep just 10% of kids from growing up in a broken home?

9. Pray together.

10. Next steps:
    - Announce next meeting.
    - Ask them to read this book.

NOTES

CHAPTER 1

1. W. Bradford Wilcox, "The Evolution of Divorce," National Affairs, no. 1 (fall 2009), http://www.nationalaffairs.com/publications/detail/the-evolution-of-divorce. Brad Wilcox is the director of the National Marriage Project at the University of Virginia, a senior fellow at the Institute for American Values, and a professor of sociology at the University of Virginia.

2. "Children of Divorced Parents More Likely to Start Smoking," University of Toronto Media Room, posted March 14, 2013, http://media.utoronto.ca/media-releases/children-of-divorced-parents-more-likely-to-start-smoking/.

3. Associated Press, "Links Seen in Divorce, Child Illness," Eugene Register-Guard, August 13, 1990, http://news.google.com/newspapers?id=MUNWAAAAIBAJ&sjid=meoDAAAAIBAJ&pg=6840,3143860&dq=children+of+divorce+more+likely+to&hl=en.

4. "Children of Divorce More Likely to End Their Marriages," University of Utah: Newswise, posted June 27, 2005, http://www.newswise.com/articles/view/512757/.

5. On the whole, marriage has been in decline in the US (and in most post-industrial countries, especially those in Europe). The current divorce/separation rate (in the US) for couples marrying for the first time is 40%–50%. Although the number of divorces and annulments has been dropping over the last decade, so has the number of marriages. In fact, the number of marriages has declined more steeply than that of divorce. In 1960, 72% of adults in the US were married; in 2011, 51% were married—a record low. Marriage is being increasingly replaced by cohabitation, single-adult households, and other living arrangements.

A bright spot: the overall divorce rate has decreased since 1980, meaning that children born to married couples these days are more likely to grow up in intact homes.

See the following sources:

- D'Vera Cohn et al, "Barely Half of U.S. Adults Are Married—A Record Low," Pew Research Social & Demographic Trends, December 14, 2011, http://www.pewsocialtrends.org/2011/12/14/barely-half-of-u-s-adults-are-married-a-record-low/.

- Elizabeth Marquardt, David Blankenhorn, Robert I. Lerman, Linda Malone-Colón, and W. Bradford Wilcox, "The President's Marriage Agenda for the Forgotten Sixty Percent," *The State of Our Unions* (Charlottesville, VA: National Marriage Project and Institute for American Values, 2012). 67, http://nationalmarriageproject.org/.

- Richard Fry, "No Reversal in Decline of Marriage," Pew Research Social & Demographic Trends, November 20, 2012, http://www.pewsocialtrends.org/2012/11/20/no-reversal-in-decline-of-marriage/.

- "National Marriage and Divorce Rate Trends," Centers for Disease Control and Prevention: National Vital Statistics System, http://www.cdc.gov/nchs/nvss/marriage_divorce_tables.htm.

6. Ephesians 5 in particular upholds marriage as a reflection of the relationship between Jesus and the church. But this chapter (as well as other passages in Ephesians) is also about the transformational purpose of relationship, first through Jesus, then through other people.

Look at how Paul contrasts our "natural state" with what happens when we allow God to live in us supernaturally:

- Once we were darkness; now Jesus' light shines through us. (5:8)
- Once our actions were motivated by selfishness; now we want to do what pleases the Lord. (5:9-11)
- We were asleep, basically dead; now we are alive in Him. (5:14)
- We did foolish and unwise things; now our actions can be guided by true wisdom, an understanding of God's will and intent. (5:15-16)
- Once we got drunk on wine; now we can fill ourselves with joy in the Spirit. (5:18)

Jesus transforms us through salvation, but His work doesn't end there. He continues to transform us through other relationships:

- Once we treated others the way the world taught us: we lied, held grudges, and took what wasn't ours, lashing out in bitterness and rage and in every form of malice. (4:25-28,31)
- But now we treat others the way Jesus taught, handed down through generations of believers: we speak truthfully, share with those in need, and build others up, forgiving them the way God forgave us through Christ. (4:20-21,25-32)

In short, our old way of life separated us from God and ripped us apart from one another. Our new life through Jesus makes us one with God and one with others. It gives all believers a unity of purpose that we are to nurture and maintain: to become more like God. (See 4:3,24; 5:1.)

In no other relationship is that God-compelled unity more encompassing than in marriage. Physically, emotionally, and spiritually, God intends for husbands and wives to be unified.

That is why a man leaves his father and mother and is united to his wife, and they become one flesh.
(Genesis 2:24, NIV)

7. Gary L. Thomas, *Sacred Marriage: What If God Designed Marriage to Make Us Holy More Than to Make Us Happy?* (Grand Rapids, Michigan: Zondervan, 2000), 13. Kindle edition.

CHAPTER 2

8. Missional Specialist Eric Swanson, who works with Leadership Network (see **LeadNet.org**) in Dallas, has spent significant time reviewing the websites of America's 100 largest churches (identified by *Outreach Magazine*) to see what they're doing to help marriages. Swanson writes, "Of the 100 largest churches in the U.S., 36 [of the] 100 had no visible … easy-to-identify ministry to married couples …. When searching the staff page … there was no one identified with 'marriage' or 'marrieds.' " There was one bright spot in Eric's research that we want to point out: 27 of the 100 churches sponsored a date night for their people at least once a year. While this may not seem like much, our findings have revealed that church-sponsored date nights have a radical impact on couples. (We'll discuss more of this in chapter 6.) See Eric Swanson's post, "What I Learned About Marriage Ministry from the Websites of 100 Large Churches," Leadership Network, September 21, 2012, http://leadnet.org/blog/post/what_i_learned_about_marriageministry_after_looking_at_the_websites_of_outr.

9. W. Bradford Wilcox, "The Evolution of Divorce," National Affairs, no. 1 (fall 2009), http://www.nationalaffairs.com/publications/detail/the-evolution-of-divorce.

10. John Gottman and Julie Gottman, *The Marriage Survival Kit* (Philadelphia, PA: Brunner/Mazel, 1999), 304–330 as cited by Brian D. Doss, "Expanding the Reach and Effectiveness of Marital Interventions," (paper, Texas A&M University), 77, http://www.relationshipeducation.info/downloads/pdf/06%20Doss.pdf.

11. Elizabeth Weil, "Does Couples Therapy Work?" The New York Times, March 2, 2012, http://www.nytimes.com/2012/03/04/fashion/couples-therapists-confront-the-stresses-of-their-field.html?pagewanted=all&_r=2&.

CHAPTER 3

12. Sandy M. Fernandez, "History of the Pink Ribbon," Think Before You Pink, accessed November 6, 2013, http://thinkbeforeyoupink.org/?page_id=26.

13. "Breast Cancer Facts & Figures 2013-2014," American Cancer Society, accessed November 6, 2013, http://www.cancer.org/acs/groups/content/@research/documents/document/acspc-040951.pdf.

14. "Cancer Trends Progress Report, 2011/2012 Update," National Cancer Institute, http://progressreport.cancer.gov/doc_detail.asp?pid=1&did=2011&chid=102&coid=1016&mid.

15. Stephanie Chen, "Could You Be 'Infected' by Friend's Divorce?" *CNN Living*, June 10, 2010, http://www.cnn.com/2010/LIVING/06/10/divorce.contagious.gore/index.html.

16. In 2008, women bought 74% of all books on family and relationships. In 2010, they made 62% of all book purchases in the US. To read more, see:

- Kiri Blakely, "Self-Help Books: Why Women Can't Stop Reading Them …," *Forbes*, June 10, 2009, http://www.forbes.com/2009/06/10/self-help-books-relationships-forbes-woman-time-marriage.html.
- *2012 U.S. Book Consumer Demographics & Buying Behaviors Annual Review* (New Providence, NJ: Bowker Market Research & Publishers Weekly, 2012) as cited by Bowker in "Generation Y Leads in Book Buying, Says Industry's Most Comprehensive Report," http://www.bowker.com/en-US/aboutus/press_room/2012/pr_08142012.shtml.

CHAPTER 4

17. Dr. Shawn Stoever is the co-author of two books, *The Wholehearted Marriage: Fully Engaging Your Most Important Relationship* and *5 Days to a New Marriage*. You can read about Shawn at **WinShapeRetreat.org** and about the WinShape Foundation at **WinShape.org**.

18. To help you create larger group experiences, we have designed resources just for you. Easy to use (think: *Just add water*) and ready to be edited and adapted as you see fit:

- For single Larger Group Experiences, go to marriedpeople.org/largergroups/.
- For a four-pack of Larger Group Experiences (a year's worth, called MarriedPeople Annual Strategy Pack), go to marriedpeople.org/strategypack/.
- For the most updated list of resources, go to **MarriedPeople.org**.
- For games, see downloadyouthministry.com/games.

CHAPTER 5

19. We have used the Lees' story with their permission.

20. See "Who Is Active in 'Group' Expressions of Faith? Barna Study Examines Small Groups, Sunday School, and House Churches," Barna Group, posted June 28, 2010, https://www.barna.org/barna-update/faith-spirituality/400-who-is-active-in-group-expressions-of-faith-barna-study-examines-small-groups-sunday-school-and-house-churches - .Ue7mplOhsmU.

21. For more details about the *5 Days to a New Marriage* resources, go to 5daystoanewmarriage.com/.

22. Shawn Stoever, email message to author, November 11, 2013. Multiple research samplings conducted by Stoever and others at WinShape Foundation have found that 78%–84% of couples who participate in these marriage intensives are still married and have increased marital satisfaction two years after their intensive experience.

23. Here are some resources you may wish to check out, particularly if you want to offer marriage-related materials to small groups:
    - For MarriedPeople Small Group Studies, go to marriedpeople.org/smallgroups/.
    - For the MarriedPeople Annual Strategy Pack (an annual subscription, which includes one Small Group Study each year, among other resources), go to marriedpeople.org/strategypack/.

CHAPTER 6

24. Katie Garvert, email message to author, 2013. See https://www.woodmenvalley.org/index.cfm/pageid/1583 for more on Woodmen Valley Chapel and its special need ministries.

25. Our resources that may help you in this area:

- For MarriedPeople Can't Wait Dates, go to http://marriedpeople.org/kits/.
- For MarriedPeople E-ZINE (monthly emails), see http://marriedpeople.org/ezine/.
- For the MarriedPeople Annual Strategy Pack (an annual subscription, which includes four Dates and Down the Road mentoring resources, among other resources), go to marriedpeople.org/strategypack/.

26. As you may have read in chapter 2, there was one bright spot in Eric's research that we pointed out: 27 of the 100 largest churches in the US sponsored a date night for their people at least once a year. While this may not seem like much, our findings have revealed that church-sponsored date nights have a radical impact on couples.

27. To read more about the National Marriage Project, go to nationalmarriageproject.org/about/.

28. W. Bradford Wilcox and Jeffrey Dew, *The Date Night Opportunity: What Does Couple Time Tell Us About the Potential Value of Date Nights?* (Charlottesville, VA: National Marriage Project and Institute for American Values, 2012).14. http://nationalmarriageproject.org/wp-content/uploads/2012/05/NMP-DateNight.pdf.

29. MarriedPeople and The reThink Group, Inc. MarriedPeople Survey. Marriedpeople.org, The reThink Group, Inc., April 2010–September 2013. Unpublished.

30. Timothy Keller with Kathy Keller, *The Meaning of Marriage: Facing the Complexities of Commitment with the Wisdom of God* (New York: Dutton, Penguin Group USA, Inc., 2011), 87. Kindle edition.

31. John Gottman has conducted 40 years of research on marriage and divorce. He has published numerous academic articles and

is an award-winning author. You can read more about him at gottman.com/about-us-2/dr-john-gottman/.

32. John M. Gottman and Nan Silver, *The Seven Principles for Making Marriage Work* (New York: Three Rivers Press, 1999), 47. Kindle edition.

33. The gloo app is available for smart phones on the App Store and on Google Play. To sign up, download gloo and enter the following code: c542. This will take you directly to MarriedPeople Can't Wait Dates. If you already have gloo, MarriedPeople Can't Wait Dates are located at: home menu / Champions (all) / Date Night / under Programs.

34. Create your own date night campaign for your church or community and engage your couples with relevant relationship enrichment content. Go to **DateNightWorks.com** to get started.

35. To see a sample of the MarriedPeople E-ZINE, go to marriedpeople.org/ezine/.

36. Nara Schoenberg, "Can We Talk?" *Chicago Tribune*, January 14, 2011, http://articles.chicagotribune.com/2011-01-14/features/sc-fam-0111-talk-relationship-20110111_1_happy-marriages-couples-marital-therapy.

CHAPTER 7

37. "Walking," *Wikipedia*, last modified July 10, 2013, http://en.wikipedia.org/wiki/Walking.

CHAPTER 8

38. For more on Grace Community Church, check out their website at **Grace-sa.org**.

CHAPTER 9

39. Shaunti Feldhahn, email message to author, January 8, 2014.

40. We have used the Butlers' story with their permission.

41. Pablo S. Torre, "How (and Why) Athletes Go Broke." *SI Vault*, March 23, 2009, http://si.com/vault/article/magazine/MAG1153364/5/index.htm.

CHAPTER 10

42. If you want more details about our resources, visit **MarriedPeople.org** for an up-to-date list. We also think these organizations do a great job at providing ready-to-use resources:

- re | engage Marriage Enrichment Program, Watermark Community Church, Dallas, Texas. To read more about re | engage, visit **MarriageHelp.org**.
- HomeWord Center for Youth and Family. For details, visit **HomeWord.com**.

ACKNOWLEDGEMENTS

It seems a little silly to us that our two names are the only ones that appear on the cover of this book. Our names don't represent the number of hearts and minds that contributed to this work. So many people have poured themselves into this book and into our lives as well. We are grateful!

We would first like to thank our editor, Melanie Williams, for her brilliant direction, guiding input, and, most of all, her encouragement and cheering on of this important message. Working with one author is tough enough; two had to feel like herding cats. There were many days when we both felt like doing anything but writing, but she spurred us on. We are forever grateful.

We would also like to thank the men and women who read our early manuscript and offered helpful suggestions: Andrew Accardy, Brian Berry, Debbie Causey, Shaunti Feldhahn, Ryan Gernand, Todd Graham, Jána Guynn, Mike Kenyon, John McGee, Amanda McGuire, Jeff McLaughlin, Carey Nieuwhof, Tim Popadic, Chris Reed, Todd Olthoff, Tim Walker, and Steve Williams. Your gracious insight radically changed the nature of this book. Thanks for caring about us and for marriages. You are all amazing leaders and thinkers.

We would also like to thank the church leaders who, over the years, have trusted us enough to give us a ministry that became a laboratory to learn how to care for families and marriages. I (Ted) would like to thank Rick Warren, Doug Fields, Andy Stanley, Reggie Joiner, Bill Willits, and Joel Thomas. I (Doug) am so grateful to have been mentored by these great men: Jim Burns, Tim Timmons, and Rick Warren. Your influence in our lives has been immeasurable.

I (Ted) would like to thank the team I worked with every day at North Point: Jána Guynn, Courtney Thomas, and Sara Fogle. Your friendship, encouragement, and gifts are all over the pages of this book. I would like to thank the production team, musicians, and volunteers who worked tirelessly to create incredible environments for married couples. I would like to thank the team at Orange who make MarriedPeople more than I ever dreamed it could be: Nancy Squires, Reggie Joiner, Reggie Goodin, Susan Odom, Todd Graham, Tim Walker, Phil Pierce, Greg Payne, Ryan Boon, Hudson Phillips, Kelli Wallace, and the rest of the Orange team. I particularly would like to thank Nancy Squires. You serve our church partners with excellence, consistency, and joy.

I (Doug) am surrounded by so many amazing people who love me, push me, encourage me, support me, and ultimately accept me as friend, brother, and co-worker and allow me to do what I do. The crew at HomeWord: Andrew Accardy, Seth Bartlette, Jim Burns, Becca Burns, Dean Bruns, David Peck, Debbie Phlieger (my amazing assistant), Krista Salazar, and Cindy Ward. The gang at Downloadyouthministry.com who make me laugh like no others and make me want to actually go into an office: Jon McBerny, Josh Griffin, Matt McGill, and Parker Stech. People should not have as much fun as we do and call it "work." There're too many others who have partnered with me at Saddleback Church and Mariners Church to help me in the ways of ministry—you know who you are and I'm thankful for you. Especially grateful for my friend Fadi Cheikha, who gives me an office, won't allow me to pay for a meal, encourages me daily, and loves my family like a life-long friend. I can't find words to express my thankfulness.

Of course my (Ted) heart is overwhelmed with gratitude for my best friend and wife, Nancie, and our three children, Chapman,

Judson, and Teddie. You bring meaning to everything, including this book. My heart and head cannot contain the blessing you are in my life!

I (Doug) expressed it all in the dedication. My family means everything to me, and I'm so grateful to have a tight family that loves Jesus and one another and still likes to be with us as young adults. I'm beyond blessed.

ABOUT THE AUTHORS

Some people have found it helpful to know a bit of our stories in order to better understand why we care so deeply about helping churches help marriages.

In 1992, my (Ted) first job out of college was as the youth pastor of a Methodist church in my small hometown of Centre, Alabama. To suggest I didn't know what I was doing would be generous. Thankfully, I was just wise enough to know I didn't know what I was doing. But I was definitely eager to learn, and I attended a Youth Specialties Convention in 1993, where I sat and listened to this guy named Doug Fields talk about ministry. As Doug unpacked what would later be known as "Purpose-Driven® Youth Ministry," I was hooked. I loved the simple concept that behind everything he did for teenagers was a corresponding and intentional biblical purpose. Each action was part of a larger strategy.

A month after the convention, a friend and I attended a one-day seminar that Doug was leading in Atlanta. While I was there, I felt led to speak to Doug, but when break time hit, I changed my mind and returned to my seat. My buddy laughed at me and said, "Quit being so chicken and talk to the guy!" I lovingly said, "Shut up. I will." Finally getting up the nerve, I was about to introduce myself to Doug when a man stepped in front of me. His rude action sparked this prayer: "Okay, God, I feel like You want me to do this, but if this guy doesn't move in 30 seconds, I'm done." (For what it's worth, I don't pray those types of prayers anymore.) Right at the 30-second mark, the guy finished and it was my turn. I blurted out something that surprised even myself, "Do you have an internship program?" Doug responded graciously and with a smile and a chuckle said, "Not really, but maybe we could start one with you this summer." I returned to my seat and confidently told my friend, "I'm moving to California." He laughed and said, "Yeah, and I'm moving to Egypt." Three months later I moved to California to work with Doug and his team. My friend stayed in Alabama.

Why did I do something that everyone thought was so crazy? Because I honestly believed (and still do 20 plus years later) that no organization should be more intentional and strategic than the local church. I spent five years with Doug on staff at Saddleback Church, where I learned the powerful concept of asking why before creating activity. Then, in 1999 I relocated my family to Atlanta to work at North Point Community Church. Like Saddleback, North Point is extremely thoughtful in how they approach ministry. I share this with you because I didn't begin ministry with an intentional mindset; I started as a hungry learner who began to see that **effective ministries are strategic ministries**.

/////

I (Doug) can't tell you how thankful I am that Ted took that step of faith to ignite a conversation that has resulted in over 20 years of friendship and partnership in ministry. Despite the fact that we have lived on opposite sides of the country since 1999, we have remained dear friends. Our families have vacationed together for years, and my kids view Ted as an uncle (as his kids do me). Every time we're together our conversation migrates toward the impact and meaning of the church. I realize this isn't exciting for most people, but for us it's a common language and passion. As a lifelong youth worker, I wake up every day thinking about kids and how to help them draw closer to Jesus. But the older I get, the more

I realize that if I want to help kids, I've got to help parents, and if I'm going to help people be better parents, I better start paying attention to their marriages.

For the last few years, I've expanded my focus on youth work into youth, family, parenting, and marriage. Ever since Ted left my team to work in the marriage space at North Point, we've been dreaming about combining our energy, passions, and strengths to create a church-based strategy to help marriages. That's why you're holding this book.

We're both passionate believers that **the church is the difference maker in marriages as well as the hope of the world**. Whenever we get discouraged by how little churches are doing for married couples overall, we remind each other that it was really just a few decades ago that youth ministry (as we know it today) didn't exist. Now, youth pastors are a respected and needed hire within the church (though there is still room for improvement there too). We are optimistic it will only be a few years from now that we'll look back and say, "Remember when ministry to married couples was almost nonexistent?" That reality is not only our optimistic hope; it's our prayer.

TED LOWE

Ted Lowe is a speaker, a blogger, and the founder of MarriedPeople (**MarriedPeople.org**), the marriage division of Orange (**WhatIsOrange.org**), a company devoted to influencing the next generation. After serving as the director of MarriedLife at North Point Community Church in Alpharetta, Georgia, Ted joined the Orange team to create MarriedPeople. The mission of MarriedPeople is to help churches help marriages by giving them a proactive strategy and the resources to empower that strategy.

Ted is a graduate of Fuller Theological Seminary, in Pasadena, California. He lives in Cumming, Georgia, with his four favorite people: his wife, Nancie, and their three children. For more information about Ted and MarriedPeople, visit **MarriedPeople. org** or join them on Facebook at **facebook.com/marriedpeople** or Twitter **@Married_People.**

DOUG FIELDS

Doug Fields is the Executive Director for the HomeWord Center for Youth and Family at Azusa Pacific University (**HomeWord.com**). He's an award-winning author of more than 50 books, including *7 Ways to Be Her Hero, Refuel,* and *Getting Ready for Marriage.* He's the co-founder of **DownloadYouthMinistry.com** and is in constant demand as a speaker and ministry consultant. He has also served on staff at two incredible churches in Southern California for a combined 30 years (Mariners Church and Saddleback Church).

He is happily married to his wife of 30 years, Cathy, and they are parents of three young adults: Torie, Cody, and Cassie. More information about Doug is available at **DougFields.com**.